Uncle Neal's (Curious) Rainy Day Book

Stories to Enliven Your Day

Neal Fridley

Published by the author
Neal Fridley
p.o. box 1563
Port Angeles,WA 98362

First Edition, 2016

This book is dedicated to my folks who somehow made me into a traveler, to my dear wife who wished I would stay at home more, yet enabled my wanderings with love, and to the Mount Pleasant campfire crew who has been my audience for many a tall tale told around the campfire.

Warning: These stories are made of insubstantial stuff. They are lightweight, like marshmallows, and like marshmallows, too many eaten at one sitting are unsatisfying. Therefore I strongly recommend reading one or two at a time. Rainy days are perfect. Not only do you get something to do, you get a pick-me-up. However, you have been warned of a SURFEIT OF FLUFF.

A man may forget his way home,
Yet still recall his first bicycle

Haiku by Kathyrn Fridley

Contents

*The Dirt is the name of my property. Ben Cartwright of the TV show Bonanza had The Ponderosa. My spread is named The Dirt.

Mas Novocain, por favor.

A Dental vacation in Sunny Mexico

My trip to Mexico got started when I broke a tooth on a Triscuit. Now, I hold no grudge against the fine people at Nabisco. I am sure they are just doing their job, making snack crackers out of oat hulls and chaff, but I do hold a grudge against the medical and insurance people, who have conspired to demand a week's wages for a crown on a tooth.

I visited my dentist, with whom I have a cash-and-carry business relationship, and after he noodled around in my mouth with that little nut pick thing, he announced the verdict; "You're going to need a crown, my friend, about $800 worth." He mistook my gagging response for a need to rinse and spit, but really I was choking on the price.

I went home to my wife and ranted about this latest injustice, "I could fly down to Mexico, get my tooth fixed, and live like a Saudi Prince at the Hotel Presidente for a week and still come back money ahead." After further venting, I went to bed to forget about it. In the morning I found a stack of print-outs beside the computer, topped with a post-it that said "Baboo, Be careful what you ask for. Here is your dental vacation itinerary in Mexico." And there it was; she had searched the internet for "Dentist in Mazatlan" and found a retired American named Arthur Griffin who had married a Mexican woman who was a dentist. Arthur had written an article for a retirees website describing his experiences as an expatriate in Mexico. He closed his story with some comments about the low cost of medical and dental services in Mexico and an offer to help to anyone wanting dental work done.

Now I had to put my money where my mouth was. I could stay home and spend $800 for the crown, but I also needed my teeth cleaned and I needed new lenses in my glasses plus the required eye exam. Those bills would add up to $1000, and that became my budget. Surely I could find a cheap place to stay in Mazatlan, use up some bonus air miles, and cover the optometrist and dental bills in Mexico for less than $1000.

I sent out an e-mail to a number of my friends titled "Brilliant idea #436" describing my plan and hoping to find someone to come with me on this jaunt. The most positive response I got was one that read, "I'll wait for brilliant idea #437", so I went solo.

In Sunny Mexico

In Mazatlan you step out of the airplane directly into shocking glare, humidity, and heat. You are allowed a respite in the relative cool of the airport before you have to run the gauntlet of time-share touts and taxi hustlers lined up outside. Shuttle vans run into town with 6 or 7 passengers for a reasonable $5.50. The catch is that you can not take one back to the airport. Taxis only, and the price is $25.

The vacationers who boarded the airport shuttle with me were all headed to resort hotels and time-share beachfront condos, but the driver chose to drop me off first. My apartment was only four blocks from hotel row but still farther off the beaten path than most will venture during their stay. The courtyard encompassing my apartment was a postcard setting, lacking only a peasant in a serape and sombrero, snoozing in the shade of a cactus (a possible job opening, if any of you are interested). I was greeted by the landlady in shorts and kneepads who, along with her son, were mixing mortar for a garden wall.

2

Apartmentos Fiesta, where I stayed, is a small compound of low buildings divided into 11 apartments and the landlady's house. As in all of Mazatlan, the buildings were made entirely of masonry; only the doors were wood. For more than twenty years the owners had labored to build walls, paths, and courtyard benches decorated with bits of pottery, tile shards and colored bottles set in mortar. Nooks and alcoves were tucked into every corner providing a place to read, sunbathe, barbecue or eat. If I was more of a gardener I could name the many tropical trees and plants. I am fairly confident in identifying the ones with coconuts attached to the top or bananas hanging on a stem, but the others are just "jungle" to me. My father could identify both kinds of flowers in the world of plants: the rose and the kistoonthia. The kistoonthia was his name for all the other flowers that weren't a rose, and that impairment continues in the male line of my family.

My room was one of the cheapest at $18 per night. The water supply was a gravity flow system from a tank on the roof. Just the basics, and only clean enough to suit the average young college student. The door was just five and a half feet high, a real head knocker for me, but the ceiling light fixture was decorated with a medallion of clam shells cemented all around it. That was typical of the whole apartment complex; real creativity and hard work went into decoration, yet the functional basics were hit and miss. The electrical service to my apartment was more primitive than last century's porcelain tube and knob wiring. I didn't worry though; I don't think the wiring could stand up to a real electrocution. If I plugged in the reading light with the frayed wire, I think the utility wires would burn out before I did.

The tourist hotel area is called the Zona Dorada, or Golden Zone, I suppose in acknowledgment of the huge amount of money tourists bring to an otherwise crippled economy. My contact in Mazatlan, Arthur the retired American, said that I would have no trouble getting a place to stay or a dental appointment since business was slow to non-existent. Certainly I saw dozens of restaurants open but empty every night.

I had some Mexican coins from a trip I made years ago. I offered them to a cab driver but he returned them, saying "No Valid" When the peso crashed some years ago, the government knocked three zeros off the value of the money, and the coins became worthless. My landlady decorated her mantel with invalidated coins, gluing at least a thousand of them to the wall and varnishing them. When the world hands you lemons…(glue them to your mantel)

My dental appointment was set for the next day, but I thought a little comparison shopping for dentists would be good. There were several offices along the main road and I stopped in at one. Air conditioned waiting room, pretty receptionist, magazines on a little table, and, down the corridor, a white-coated dentist. All in my comfort zone, but the price, I discovered, was $250 for a crown. Across the square I found Dr. Eduardo Garcia's office, and though the sign said "open", it was getting to be siesta time and the door was locked. I heard voices inside so I knocked. A distinguished looking dentist came to the door and let me into his office. A videotape he had been watching continued to play, displaying a Mexican cutie's face bobbing about rhythmically as she cried in a husky voice, "Dios Mio, Oh Dios, Si, *Si*, Si!" Dr. Garcia turned it off briskly and said "Now, Señor, what can I do for your teeth?" He too gave me a price of $250, though I should have asked if there was an entertainment surcharge. I opted to stay with my original choice, Arthur's wife, Maria

Arthur picked me up at a beachfront restaurant called El Shrimp Bucket and we drove to his wife's *consultoria*. I got into his dusty, battered pickup and fastened my seatbelt. The click caught Arthur's attention and he looked at me in surprise. "You're probably the only one in Mazatlan with a seatbelt on. I had forgotten the truck had any. But while we're on the subject, let me warn you; If we get in a fender-bender don't, I repeat *don't* get out of the car. If somebody smacks us I am going to step on the gas and get away from there fast, and probably the other driver will too."

"I've heard of that before", I said, but I am still shocked."

Arthur explained, "If we were foolish enough to wait around for a policeman to come, he would hold a kind of auction to see which driver was going to pay him the most money to not get a ticket. The low bidder gets stuck with a ticket regardless of whose fault it was. And lock your door while we are driving around." It was Arthur's opinion that the state of Sinaloa, where we were, had a reputation similar to New Jersey's: a seat of organized crime, and tough-minded inhabitants with a readily identifiable accent.

Arthur had been a construction worker in Alaska during oil boom times and had seen financial reverses, a back injury, and a divorce before he retreated to Mexico. I listened carefully for signs of an expatriate's cynicism or denigration of his newly-chosen country, but found little evidence of that. He admired the Mexican's struggle against hardship and he wasn't too down on America.

My dentist, Doctoria Maria Elena Flores Mendoza was friendly and pretty, but not very professional looking in her cutoff Levis, sandals, and tank top. She preferred to have her husband Arthur translate for us, but she was a *talker*! She fired Spanish words at me at 600 rounds a minute, a rate surpassed only by the Vulcan machine cannon.

Arthur had said in a prior e-mail that doctors and dentists work for *you*, putting their own agenda or the hospital's agen-

5

da in a lower priority. Several times during the procedures, Dr. Maria asked me if I wanted something done this way or that, and I wasn't used to such deference. Usually, American dentists recommend a procedure and expect you to nod your head. For instance, she asked me if I wanted her to apply some varnish to the tooth as a temporary cap until the crown would be installed two days later. "What do you recommend?" I asked. There followed a 400 word discourse from her in Spanish, at her usual high rate of delivery and volume. Arthur's translation was brief: "Whatever you want" he said. "But it tastes like hell." Wanting all the protection I could get for my tooth, I opted for the varnish, which looked suspiciously like Super Glue. It did taste awful, as bad as anything I have ever put in my mouth, and I am a man who once siphoned diesel fuel when I had the hiccups.

The consultoria, which was really an enclosed part of the carport, was shabby and dingy. The light was a single ceiling fixture, the big swing arm lamp was burned out, or only there for looks, and like all of the other fixtures, third hand. I wished there was a wash basin in the room but most likely the kitchen of the attached residence served that purpose. She did use exam gloves and there was a plastic cap over the hypodermic needle, but that was the extent of sanitary procedures. Extension cords snaked across the floor and the spittoon didn't work. A crucifix adorned one wall, along with three prints of Jesus on the cross, one a real bleeder.

She mixed up some rubbery substance in a Cool Whip tub to make a mold of my teeth. I hadn't had a crown done before but I suppose this is standard procedure. The amount that got smeared in my beard is probably not standard.

After the crown was installed, she cleaned my teeth. She put a small burr on her dental drill and skittered it all over my teeth. I'd say she removed as much enamel as tartar.

There was more to my trip than dentistry

To make the most of my visit, I had an eye exam and had new bifocal lenses made for my glasses. Total cost was $32. Pay no attention to the boys squatting in the alley behind the optometrist's office grinding the bottoms out of coke bottles.

I walked out among the many modest but very nice houses in the Golden Zone. Again, all masonry and tile roofs, all windows barred and each yard walled and gated, some with barbed wire or broken glass atop the walls. Nice, mid-price cars were kept behind garage gates and those parked on the street had a security bar clamped to the steering wheel. I was greeted at every other house by a guard dog. The Mazatlecos favor 8 lb. short-haired dogs of the mutt breed, low maintenance and hyper-yappy. You could follow my progress up one street and down the next from the racket the little varmints made.

I wish I had my camera ready when "Mr. Junk" came in to view. He was a small fellow with an imp's wild hair and goatee, tanned dark, and bare but for shorts and huaraches. He drove a thoroughly worn out three-wheeled vehicle powered by a wheezy little motorcycle engine. The surrey canopy flapped and ballooned in the breeze and a filthy plastic barrel was his cargo. I later learned from Arthur that his nickname was "Junk" in Spanish and that he raised pit bulls and was a long distance runner of local fame.

My hippie appearance still stands out in Mexico. I have heard that Mexicans are used to seeing bearded, long haired gringos, but are still not comfortable with it. The locals were without exception, trimmed and neat in their appearance. Gang wannabes were kept out of the tourist areas by policemen on bicycles. Nowhere did I see the grunge look common in Seattle. The one exception was some young American stoners who asked for spare change three times in 15 minutes without realizing they had just asked me. I have been panhandled more in the USA than in Mexico.

The world's cutest 5 year old girls offered to sell me Chiclets or beg a coin. They could have been poster girls for UNICEF. As I passed by ten minutes later, they appeared to be on top of their game, having an ice cream cone break at curbside.

Traffic on the main roads looked dangerous and chaotic, but there is more headlight and taillight glass littering the intersections of Seattle than I saw in Mazatlan. Still, the loneliest guy in town isn't the Maytag repairman, it is the guy who sells turn indicator replacement bulbs. Boombox cars passed by now and then as in America, but I never saw or heard the exhibitionist tire-screecher or street racer.

Along hotel row there are public access paths to the beach between the jammed-together restaurants and hotels. I often packed a few cold beers and walked down to the beach to watch the sunset. A young man who had spent the day selling horse rides to tourists on the beach cantered home, riding proudly as a cavalryman on parade. Three musicians, accordion, base and guitar, chose to walk the peaceful beach on their way to an evening restaurant gig. The sunset was a fine background for this picture, like a gold coin dropping into a slot on the horizon. Sunset is also the perfect hour for watching pelicans gliding among the palms.

Bottled water was available for delivery to my apartment. Just leave $1.50 under the empty 5 gallon jug outside the door and the next time you look the jug is full. The tap water is OK for washing, but at peak demand hours the pressure is zero. I was sipping an innocent glass of orange juice one morning sitting in the shady court of a nice restaurant, when the ice delivery man pulled

8

up in his van. Ice is delivered to the restaurant in 150 lb. blocks, far too heavy to lift, so the delivery man swings it to the ground with ice tongs and skids it on the sidewalk to the service door. I looked at the chipped ice in my drink and figured that, health-wise, I might as well lick the pavement. ♫ Down on the Rancho Grande we have the Diarrheeeeeya.. Ay, yi yi yi. ♪ ♪

The central district is a mix of locals and tourists. The central mercado is a vast, roofed area housing florists, fruit and vegetable sellers, and one long row exclusively for butchers. I admired the skill it takes to start with a stiff cow (with tail) and turn it into a neat display of perfectly sliced steaks, not that this would be a selling point if they tried it a my local Safeway.

I'd like to say that I roamed far and wide, exploring and savoring, but the hundred degree heat and high humidity defeated me. Mazatlan was having an extended summer, not an el niño nor an un-niño, more of an in-betweeño. So when I got the crown installed I called it quits and bought the next ticket home.

I had tried for several days to find an alternative to the $25 taxi fare to the airport. The cheap, chicken-coop-on-the-roof buses let you off two sweltering miles from the airport, but in the end my landlady, who had been so helpful, said that she could drive me to the airport for $20 and the money would really help their limited budget. Then I was glad to pay up.

Anyway, the tooth is fixed and I'm back in the corner of the world I love. If there is a down side to my new tooth it is the radio signals it brings in. As I type this, if I hold my mouth just right, I can hear a disc jockey exclaiming "Radio X-E-R-B, Mucho Musica para Tijuana !"*

Carramba!,

Neal

*Shame, shame! I had a perfectly truthful story going until I had to go stick that in.

Some names have been changed to protect me from ticked-off Mexican Dentists.

I search for Ireland: I'll start by looking in all the pubs I can find.

This is a journal about an ordinary trike touring trip that ran off the rails. As you will see, the challenges overwhelmed us; we abandoned our trikes and traveled by bus for most of the trip.

My traveling companions Rebecca and George came to Port Angeles for a good visit and a test ride. It was great to see them after so many years and chapters in our lives. I had last seen them only briefly in 2009 and before that I would have to go back to 1968 when we were all so much younger and fit.

I need someone to watch my back nowadays. In fact I need someone to watch my front, too. Parkinson's disease makes me a target for pickpockets and muggers. I am the old, lame antelope in the herd surrounded by hungry predators. Or I would be if I didn't believe in the basic goodness of most people. I suppose I shouldn't even be going on this trip. It's a bit of a stretch to think my stamina and abilities are up to the job. But the alternative is to lie down and take a long nap. So I keep on going. I really needed to have them see me in my present condition. I had sent them the following letter:

Full disclosure disclaimer: You should be aware of how much Parkinson's has taken from me. I can still think and express myself in writing as well as ever, but that's the only good news. My handwriting is illegible and my keyboard skills rely on spell check to write for me. I make a few garbled suggestions and spell check does the rest.

Physically:

- Half a dozen times a day I scare the hell out of myself lurching toward a fall. So far I catch myself all but 3 or 4 times a year. I need help getting up out of a very low sitting position, so don't let me near a Turkish Squatter toilet. I am installing standing-up aids on my trike. Even with a hiking stick I walk like a penguin failing a sobriety test.

- My smile and laugh muscles are disconnected, so I wear an expression like a wooden cigar store Indian.

- My once mighty stamina has slipped to that of a canary with the croup. On my Pacific coast Highway trip I averaged 35 mi/day, the slowest guy on the road. In Holland and Germany that dropped to 25 mi/ day but that was because I found so many little diversions and delights to dawdle over (a good thing). I will have to try some local bike camping to see if I can do 20 miles /day on my trike and still rise and shine the next morning. Mental:

- My spirits are good to great, though is difficult for anyone to tell (see cigar store Indian above.) Rip Knot who traveled with me for a month last year in France was very frustrated by this. I would be sitting in our rented car, happily sailing along, admiring the scenery, and not realizing what a silent lump I was being. Even when I was pickled tink it just didn't show through the gray. I just sat there like a lump on a bog.

- My judgment and common sense have slipped. Even to the point of thinking I can go bike touring like before with no problem. I got lost one night in a strange convoluted rural neighborhood all because I thought I could cover 7 miles before dark with a late afternoon start. I need a companion to go along behind me collecting my hat, walking stick, and pants I have carelessly left behind.

I didn't want them to be surprised when they saw how slow and weak I had become. I will rely on them a great deal during this trip. I had written them, truthfully but with a light heart, but seeing me wobble getting up out of a chair and how slowly I eat is a whole nother thing, as they say.

My home life will be well looked after in my absence by my wife, Kathyrn, who has stood by me these last 46 years. If the goats, chickens, and cats behave themselves and the household maintenance doesn't exceed her patience, I will return to a happy home.

I am flying Delta's Business Class, which is like first class for we mere mortals. I could never afford the steep ticket price in cash, but my wife and I have slowly piled up a heap of credit card air miles. This was certainly a good way to burn through them. My dear wife is glad to be rid of them.

Oh, the poor ticket agent I drew to book my flight! I placed a conference call with my traveling companion and spent more than three hours negotiating the complexities of getting seats. I still don't have businesses class on all legs of the trip and we have a 17 hour layover in NY.

I need more than a month to make a trip like this. I need a week to hit my stride camping, getting used to sleeping on the ground in a tent, and finding where all my kit is supposed to be in my panniers. Another week or two for bum weather, lost baggage, the Plague, and other such calamities, leaving a week to enjoy doing what I came to do. If I have a run of 30 days of misfortune I would have a great story to tell. And having a story to tell is why I go.

At 37 days, I am no longer pushing on the calendar trying to slow the days down. I am ready and willing to return, a good thing.

Wheelchair service was good for me and my friends too. I needed wheelchair service because of the long distances to be covered in a hurry in the airports. My friends benefited by being led directly on the short path through the queues.

In spite of best intentions, my planning for the trip to Ireland slipped into Parkinson's mode. Not only did I fail to update my journal several times before departure, when departure day arrived I was mostly but not completely prepared. The biggest single obstacle was my trike packing and especially the battery. My problems with the battery are still not resolved as I write this in mid-November. The airlines are scared of lithium batteries. Mine are large enough to be banned from airline baggage altogether. But, I found a loophole. By separating it into 3 smaller units, they would pass. So I cut my fine, expensive battery up. The TSA probably took it for a bomb. I can't swear that they took it outside and tried to detonate it, but they might as well have; it disappeared en route.

All during the preparation process and hassles of leaving I focused on that moment when I and my traveling companions were all aboard, the engines spooled up and the plane began to roll down the runway. When that moment came, it was just as I had imagined it. In spite of the late hour I felt elated, and then very sleepy. Come what may (and it sure did), I was on to an new chapter.

Best advice so far : In inclement weather sit snug inside a cozy pub and chat with the locals. On a fine, sunny day, sit outside a country pub and chat with the locals.

A journey of 10.000 miles begins with a trip to an ATM

What? Me? Get a little rattled at boarding time? Like when I tried to use a Burger King receipt as a boarding pass.

My neighbors, the Leprechauns, turned out to wish me Slán a fhágáil (Farewell)

Our plane taxis out to the runway. So many of us travelers feel the weight of months of planning lifting from their shoulders it is a wonder that the plane can get airborne at all.

Our modular seats gave us plenty of leg room with no one hogging the armrest next to you. Best of all they slide down into a cocoon that gives me a comfy night's sleep. I need all the help I can get fighting jetlag.

We used Delta Skylounge on our 17 hr. layover. We had peace, showers, snacks, but no place to sleep.

Baggage arrived fubar in Dublin. My bagged disassembled trike looked like a sorry sack of junk when I retrieved it at Dublin's airport. My heavy canvas bag had caught in baggage handling machinery and small parts leaked out of the rents. My fairing had been crushed into bits. With a heavy heart, I gathered up the remains and carted it out to the taxi ranks.

All of our baggage made a heap more than one taxi could carry. One enterprising taxi driver (pirate) quickly enlisted the help of a confederate and soon we were jaunting on our way to Isaac's hostel in the center of Dublin. On arrival we were informed that the charge would be 45 Euros, to which George replied, "Each?" This was too much for our venal old driver. "Aye," he answered, quick as thought. So we paid four times too much for our experience. In hindsight we should have waited for a van sized-taxi and paid the going rate of 24 euros.

After we finally rode out of Dublin, it didn't take too many miles to see that the roads were narrow, with absolutely no shoulder, and often crowded with buses. When we had the luxury of low traffic, we were faced with the second persistent problem: stone walls backed by hedges. There are tens of thousands of miles of stacked stone walls, put up in the days of horse carts, and accordingly narrow lanes. We were caught between the road edge and the din of traffic. Lying low as we did on our trikes, we had to stop, stand up and look over the wall, prairie dog fashion, to get our bearings.

We encountered a few conventional cycle tourists who were able to cope, but our trikes with trailers were too wide for safety.

We were sitting in the town of Enfield not far out of Dublin in a heap of despair. Should we soldier on? Should we retreat to Dublin and stash our bikes? I had already visited the main bus terminal in Dublin and pleaded with the station master to let me put my trike and trailer in the cargo bay of one of their large coaches. He looked at me as if I were daft and patiently explained that even if it could fit, it would surely be damaged or cause damage to other baggage, and so with a "There's a good fellow" he concluded my interview.

So it was with a low expectation of success I tried again in Enfield when a bus pulled up to a stop across the road. The driver demurred at first, but then said "I've a few minutes left in me schedule. You can give it a try." Snap to attention! All hands on deck! I roused George and Becky and we turned to. We shifted and consolidated the baggage aboard and nested our two trikes, three trailers and George's bicycle in jig time and reported in to the astonished driver with beaming faces and refreshed attitudes that we would very much like to go to Galway with him in his fine bus, if he pleased. I count that episode as my best contribution to the success of our trip.

We arrived in Galway in the middle of Friday night rush hour traffic and were directed to a campground several miles out of the city. We arrived to find a large crowded windblown caravan park beside the busy road. Fortunately we met a young man who knew what we wanted and he directed us around a corner to his parents' private campground. It was quiet, sheltered, green, and cheap at $9.00 /night. There we made our base camp, with bus trips out into Galway and the surrounding counties. Bonus! When we stayed away overnight we were not charged, though our tents and trikes remained in place.

In addition to pub food I found Thai, pizza, Indian, deli, but no Mexican, a bit of a shock to a west coast American. Some-one should open a taco stand in good old Dublin. In B and B s I looked forward to the full Irish cooked breakfast; beans, toast, black and white pudding, blanched tomato, mushrooms, bangers. hash browns, eggs cooked one way (fried firm.) Well, maybe not the warm, scalded tomato.

The gods of weather grinned for us. Our first three weeks were spent without rain, definitely not the usual rain every other day. We didn't have to break camp once in the rain.

As in France, I felt so well looked after in Ireland. In fact it was a little disconcerting to have strangers ask me "Are you OK?" or "Are you sorted?" when I must have seemed dazed and confused. Once when my rig had gotten so crossed up in traffic I just had to stand back and figure out my next move. A young man appeared and asked me, "Have you had a bang?".

On my first day riding in Irish traffic I was hugging the right lane to stay clear of faster traffic. A polite policeman stopped me to tell me to use the slow lane (which in Ireland is the left lane). Well, Duh!, dummy.

In Dublin and Galway every sidewalk eventually narrowed to a pinch point very difficult to extract myself from. Our worst experience with this occurred riding through Galway's Terror Tunnel. I inadvertently put myself in a jam by riding on a sidewalk through an underpass with a blind curve and heavy, fast traffic, when the sidewalk tapered to such narrowness that I was stopped. I should have dismounted and pulled my rig backwards until I had room enough to turn it all around, but Rebecca saw my plight and stepped out into the traffic to get me sorted out. It was so dangerous, tears of terror came to her eyes. It was one of those cross your fingers, hold your breath moments.

I spent my last night in Dublin alone...well, almost alone. I asked the hostel desk clerk for a cheap room. Yes, he had a bed in an 8 bunk dorm. I didn't care, it was for only one night and the place was full. I tossed my gear on the unoccupied bunk and left to resume work on my trike. I returned after dinner to discover that my roomies were 6 lovely young ladies. Two from Brazil, three from France and one gorgeous redheaded Brit. I asked them where they had found to have dinner, where they were from etc., the usual 'getting to know a stranger' questions. One of the Brazilians said "We would love to talk with you, but we are getting dressed now to go out for the evening", and indeed that was so. Dresses had been unpacked and hung up. Accessories littered the room. "Go ahead, don't let me keep you, I said. "I'll just crawl into my bunk here and face the wall." That suited them just fine. And true to my word I lay there, eyes closed....all the better to hear the snap of an elastic waistband on taut skin, the slither of nylon hose being drawn over young thighs. Good night, girls. Have a good time and stay safe.

The Road Goes Ever On And On.

Dear friends,

I just returned from a trip from my home in northern Washington to California. I took the scenic route down, going out to the Hoh Rain Forest on highway 101. Bright and sunny! A rain forest with no rain, what a gyp. This was the time to go; I had the road to myself for miles at a time. Somewhere in central Oregon the highway lifts 800 feet above the ocean, giving a view of 30 miles of beach, ocean and breaking surf. I'm surprised someone hasn't set up a tent and a sign : "Church of the Awesome Outdoors". The guy sitting on the stone wall playing a button accordion was me.

I have developed a few little rituals on these trips. I stop in at Katie's smokehouse in Trinidad for some "soft and oily" and then walk out to the beach to dip my toes in the Pacific. Another waypoint is my cousin Dave's store, The Liquor Still, a good place to sit back and watch "The Dave Show". Inside the store, customers were standing at the counter, money in hand, waiting to pay for their booze and smokes. Outside, Dave and a few other idlers were gathered around an ice chest admiring a fine, fat bass.

Customer: "Hey, how long you gonna be out there?"

Dave: "Keep your shorts on. You ain't got anything to do but kill time. Come check out this bass."

Dave's employee could have waited on the customers, but he was outside looking at the bass too. Before I had a chance to

speak with Dave , a sweet-faced young woman with dark chocolate brown skin walked in. She turned out to be a topless dancer
from the Tip Top club south of Eureka. She was off work due to
an on-the-job injury. She was "working the pole" upside down
when she slipped and hurt her neck. "That pole can get awful
slippery", she said. I couldn't hear her conversation with Dave,
but it looked like a negotiation for a lap dance in the store, or
maybe he was telling her about the bass. Shawn , Dave's employee starts his shift by opening a quart of beer which he swigs at
regularly and keeps ready at hand under the counter. He could
keep it in the cooler, but I don't think it has a chance to warm up
much before he opens the next one. After the dancer left, Shawn
struck up a conversation with a pal who had the same "parole vi-
olator" look as Shawn. They decided they had to leave for a few
minutes to take care of an errand. Dave said, "Go ahead. You
don't do much except loaf while you're behind the counter anyway, but hurry back because I have to pick up my son at daycare".
Shawn and his pal were gone about 5 minutes when they called
to say they had been in a wreck and wouldn't be back until the
tow truck came. It wasn't clear who was driving, but Shawn had a
long record of DUI's and his pal looked like he was catching up.
Dave tossed me the keys to the store, assured me that running the
store was a snap, zipped out the door to go pick up his kid, and
that's how I became a clerk for a while at a liquor store in Arcata

My visit with Mom was good and she was doing fine. We
went out to the cemetery to check out Pop's newly installed grave
stone. It was also an opportunity to give Pop a progress report
on my house building project. A few steps away his brother Bob
lies buried. His marker has my aunt Dorie's name on it as well,
with her date of birth and a blank space waiting to be inscribed
when she gets around to dying, though she could walk the 5 miles
to the cemetery at a brisk pace.

On the road again

Drive out to Ferndale sometime. It's a pleasant Victorian town, and the home of the original Kinetic Sculpture race. It is also the beginning of the Wildcat Road, which leads to Northern California's famous Lost Coast. The Lost Coast will stay lost as long as its main access remains a one lane road tucked behind Antonini's cow barn at the edge of town. Still, I cannot imagine how so many miles of ocean shore and grazing land has remained so sparsely populated. I saw only a few long established ranch houses and barns along the way.

Fridley pushes on for Covelo, fails to win through.

After some visits and family business in the SF Bay Area, I turned north for home. I can stand only so much of   I-5, so I found a road north of Sacramento that appeared to cross the coast range to Highway 101. The farmland and foothills in that direction looked green and inviting, so I went. After 20 miles of scattered farmhouses, the scenery gave way to oak covered knolls, cattle and redwing blackbirds stationed on every tenth fence post. I passed a sign: Covelo Road Closed, but it had been bolted in place for years. A gas station attendant had told me about this back on the Interstate, adding that it was known to be untrue and that the sign was left there by the county to discourage excess traffic. I began to feel uneasy that I hadn't seen another vehicle for an hour when I spotted two men having lunch by their yellow county truck. They were happy to advise me of the road conditions, though they laughed at my gas station road map. "It doesn't even have where we are on it", one said, "but I can tell it to you easier than drawing it on a map. Just keep going up this road 'til you get to where Gus and Squeeks have been working. They got a bright green loader and a 'dozer up where

21

the road forks. The upper road is the main road, but you'll never get through that in your van. We just come back from up there and the snow's a foot deep. But if you take the right hand fork, you'll be on a Forest Service road that mostly stays lower than the snowline. You might be able to get through on that, I don't know. Just turn right at that green loader. You can't miss it."

You may ask why I didn't turn back then and there. The answer is that Covelo has a place in my family history as the remotest godforsakenest nowhere a person could land in. But that is where my mother's family holed up during the worst years of the depression, out of money and out of luck, living on beans, oatmeal, and some creative poaching. I wanted to visit the place my mother's family struggled so hard to leave.

My mother was the first to escape, thanks to her relatively well-fixed grandmother in Eureka. Her grandmother had offered to put up my mother, send her through college and civilize her if she would have it. After graduating High School my mother packed her few belongings and boarded the motor stage down to where the railroad runs through the Eel River valley. Her head must have been spinning, because she forgot to take her stage and train fare. In a panic she admitted her mistake to the stage driver, who turned around and drove her back to the house for the money.

It was a hot day down at the isolated road junction, so my mother took off her dress and went for a swim in one of the deep pools of the river. She has always been cool in an emergency, but when the train came chuffing and hooting around the bend, she scrambled up the bank, pulling her dress on as she ran to flag down the train. The engineer braked the train, probably just to marvel at the sight of a drippy, breathless 17 year old girl trying to hide her embarrassment.

After telling me this story, mom told me that Covelo wasn't much then and probably wasn't much now. I wanted to give her the firsthand report.

I came to where the road forks. In fact it was a confusing four-way fork, but no bright green loader or bulldozer in sight. Gus and Squeeks had moved on, or had been abducted by aliens, or perhaps those two guys with the yellow county truck were Gus and Squeeks, having a laugh on me. So little in life is certain.

The two-lane had ended ten miles back and here the pavement ended. I picked one of the forks that looked promising and drove on, feeling a little more doubtful with every mile. I could see that I was coming to the crest of a ridge and, hoping to see a clear way ahead, I pushed on. The view from the top revealed yet another ridge across the valley, higher and white with snow. The down grade ahead of me was steep and mushy. If I went any further, the van wouldn't be coming back up that hill until the dry season. A clearing nearby was marked with a hand lettered sign: "Bear Wallow". I turned back at Bear Wallow; Covelo will wait for another time

A few snapshots along the way

When an AgCat crop duster buzzes you on I-5, the whole line of traffic skooches down in their seats and wobbles a little to the left.

Highway 299 from Redding to Eureka is well paved, but is so twisty a snake couldn't get over it. Along the way, search teams were looking for a body in the Trinity river.

In Del Norte County the Hiouchi River, clear green and white with foam, looked like very powerful hydrotherapy. Enticing, but what had happened to the person the searchers were looking for along the Trinity?

My van ran down the road like a scared deer for most of the trip, but the alternator light came on in Portland. I found a cheap motel to stay for the night and removed the alternator, breaking a seized bolt in the process. The next hour I spent drilling and hammering on the alternator in my room, sometimes lying under the van out in the parking lot with tools spread all over, hoping the manager wouldn't come by. I got it fixed, but don't try this in a decent motel.

As you can see, it was a highly enjoyable and educational trip. You are invited to join me on the next one.

Your pal,

Neal

p.s. This Is from Kathyrn: My "builder " is back on the job of hammering our garage/studio together. It must have been the long phone conversation Harley our cat had with Neal mid-trip. I can assure you that Harley had a heap of "yeow-yeows" with which to bend poor Neal's ear about getting home. What Neal doesn't say in his "the road runs ever on" story is that the more serious, non frolicsome goal of his California journey was to be with his Mom and my sister/family to lend continuing support as our families recover from the loss of two parents in the past year.

Kathyrn

Neal's No-good Terrible Awful Rotten Day

7:00 Awakened to find water pipes frozen up. Used brand-name bottled water to make coffee, cat's bowl being next option.

7:20 Switched over to on-board water tank to do last night's dirty dishes. Pump runs dry after 2 quarts.

7:30 Resolved to not fight it, get on with the rest of the day's work. Pipes will thaw in their own good time.

10:30 Pipes thawed in their own good time.

10:45 Came in for coffee break, but found 1 inch of water on the floor from overflowing kitchen sink.

11:00 Brought in shop vacuum and snorkeled out 15 gallons of spoogy water.

2:00 Turned electric heaters back on to get carpet drying.

2:10 Turned on propane back-up heater for extra effect.

2:20 Discovered blue smoke jetting out of the side of the trailer, indicating possible malfunction.

2:21 Shut down heater, tore apart flue and heater enclosure, fire extinguisher in hand.

2:30 Discovered that, over the summer, a chipmunk had built a nest in the heater and stocked it with a ten-year food supply.

4:30 Got out the last of the crispy black seeds, nuts, cat hair and grass. Re-installed heater.

5:00 Ran out of propane.

6:00 Went to bed, covers over head. Resolved to subscribe to Internet horoscope service.

Optimist's version of Neal's day.

7:00 Up and at 'em. Coffee, and early start on day's work.

11:00 Deep-cleaned carpets.

2:30 Serviced propane heater for winter ahead.

6:00 Early to bed for well-earned rest.

Your pal,

Neal

A Ride Down Highway 101

Dear Friends,

I have just returned from a bicycle trip down the Pacific coast highway from Port Angeles to San Francisco. I have been planning this trip for months, all the while wondering why I would want to do this. I have driven the coast route before and loved the views of sandy beaches curving away to a distant horizon. I wanted to hear surf pounding in rocky coves. I wanted to go on a bike trip before my knees or any other essential part gave out. I felt that the opportunity could easily slip farther away. I have enjoyed an occasional afternoon bike ride and I had a new bike that was raring to go.

I studied a few guide books and found that the coast route was a well-worn path. With the dozens of other cyclists on the road each summer I certainly wouldn't be alone.

I peeked into a book on training for long distance riding. It proposed a 6 month training regimen for a trip like mine, far longer than I would spend on the whole trip! I closed that book and never looked at it again. I would simply do what I could each day. One sunny morning I rode my bike out of the driveway and stayed away a long time.

Sept. 7. My friend Devan accompanied me on the first day of the trip. He is thirty, fit, and fast, so I just concentrated on riding at my own pace to get through the first day, a hilly 38 mile ride to Lake Crescent in Olympic National Park. My guidebook described the stretch of Highway 101 along Lake Crescent as narrow, winding and extremely dangerous. I didn't want to end up among the squashed bugs on the grille of a logging truck so we decided to take the Spruce Railroad Trail, an alternate route. The trail is steep, rocky, and cut with large tree roots. A few unavoidable brushes with overhanging poison oak leaves justified a wash and skinny-dip in the lake. Devan was first in and said "Come on in, the water's fine." Is there an older joke than this? (Please sign my petition to rename it Glacier Lake. It could save lives!)

My wife, Kathyrn, met us at the campground that first night and prepared a farewell meal far superior to anyone else's camp fare: a juicy steak, baked potato, hot cheese bread, and cold beer. After dinner Devan took the county bus back to Port Angeles and Kathyrn and I tried unsuccessfully to get some sleep. I was bone tired at the end of a hard first day of cycling, yet slept poorly on my camp mattress. Kathyrn gave up sleeping outside and spent a cramped night in the car.

Sept. 8. Breakfast was a happier event: fried potatoes, onions, mushrooms and scrambled eggs. She left after breakfast, both of us quiet and resigned to parting for such a long time. I concentrated on organizing all the stuff that had to go in my panniers. As soon as I was ready a few raindrops fell. The weather had been perfect for weeks prior to my leaving and I was sure the shower that began on that second morning would be brief. I was wrong; it rained every day for the next 11 days. Today was the start of a pattern soon to be familiar: rain suit on until I was hot and wet, rain suit off until I was cold and wet. I took shelter wherever I could when a real gully-washer passed over.

A few miles into my second day I followed a sign pointing to a bike route off the highway. It led miles out of my way into uninhabited forest. I came to an unmarked fork in the road and pedaled 3 miles in the wrong direction until the road ended at a remote farm with a big dog guarding it. I spent a steamed and ticked-off hour getting back to Highway 101.

My return to the highway was happily timed to meet two amazing cyclists. Paul and Reto, two young Swiss men, were on a trip worthy of a book. They had flown with their bikes to Prudhoe Bay, Alaska, starting their journey there because you can't get any farther north. Their destination was Tierra del Fuego, Argentina, the end of the world for overland travelers. We stopped together long enough to exchange stories. They thought I was the most unusual American they had met. They thought few Americans would tour by bicycle; and none at my age. Nor did they fit my image of the Swiss. Their outgoing personalities and sense of humor were a surprise to me. They had fast touring bikes and high quality gear. In spite of their bulky loads they were knocking off 70-80 miles per day. I had a chance to ride with them for a mile and I can tell you that their legs pounded the pedals like pile drivers. They pedaled downhill, which I never did (I regard it as a God-given chance to rest.) Uphill, when I shifted to my low granny gear they stood up and honked. After saying goodbye they swept out of sight in seconds. They expected to accomplish their feat in six months, and I believe they will.

An hour short of Forks I ran out of energy and daylight, so was forced to bush-camp in a brushy area off the highway. It was bad enough to camp tired and wet, but laying low in fear of being rousted made it worse.

Sept. 9 When I conceived this trip I was unwilling to make any great claims about how far I would go. I said, "to Forks or Bust. After that I'll go until it isn't fun anymore." On this soppy third morning I made good on the Forks claim, but I was a pretty downhearted traveler. I found a laundromat where I could dry my wet gear and a café that specialized in feeding large portions of fried food to hungry men. Soon I was fit for the road.

I met a cyclist who had spent 14 months on the road criss-crossing 5 western states and Hawaii. He speculated aloud that maybe it was time for him to go home. I advised him not to make any hasty decisions.

I was ready for a touch of civilization at the end of this day, so chose to stay at the Bates Motel . No, I mean the Rain Forest Hostel. The building was a run-down rambler with a garage converted to a bunk room. The proprietor was a quiet man, introverted enough to make me uncomfortable. He was certainly no housekeeper, but $6 got me a place to pitch my tent and access to the kitchen, shower, and laundry. I was the only guest that night and one of only a few that month. As spooky as the host was I could tell by all his fishing gear and photos that he was really OK. Yet the next morning I observed something that still has me wondering. I saw him standing in his back yard rhythmically flailing his forearms against a large post in front of him. This went on for more than a minute. Why would he do that? His habit had left a shiny spot on the post.

Sept. 10 For a hundred miles, Highway 101 is a slot cut through forest, alternating with views of vast clear-cut tracts. It is hilly, but with a good rideable shoulder and only the occasional passing logging truck to shower me with spray from the wet road. I was ready for a change of scenery and at Ruby Beach I got a welcome view of the Pacific.

I stopped to talk with a cyclist who was fixing a flat tire. Actually two flats. He had a puncture the day before and, in the attempt to patch it, had ruined the tube. He had taken the county bus 70 miles to the nearest bike shop, bought the wrong size tube and ruined it when installing it. Somehow the other tire had gone flat too, split at the valve stem and unrepairable. He was on his first bike trip and had never repaired a flat before. I had no magic to offer for two tubes leaking at the stem. Seeing that he was a sensitive type, and probably ready for a good cry, I wished him good luck and cleared out. In hindsight I should have offered him a slosh of the scotch I keep for just such personal low spots.

Speaking of low points, I was coming up on one myself. I had entered the Quinault Indian Reservation, as lonely a stretch as I would encounter on the whole trip. The rain had been gaining strength all day until I was completely halted, blindly peering through rain splashed glasses, disgusted, and wishing for a dry place to sleep. I bushwhacked my way off the road for a night of stealth camping, taking care to go unseen by passing drivers. Three hundred yards from the highway I found a clearing and in closing darkness and hard rain I put up my tent and fell into my sleeping bag, not moving for an hour. My Wal-Mart tent and plastic rain fly whipped and flapped and tried to fly off to the next county in the gale. I was very hungry, but cooking a hot meal in that storm was impossible. After rummaging in my kit I found a camper's squeeze tube of peanut butter and jelly I had mixed at home. I sucked on that until it was gone. Even now that seems like a treasure I profoundly enjoyed. When it was gone I lay back and decided that the bears could come eat me if they wanted to, and I was confident in the knowledge that the only intruder who would ever find me on such a night would be a serial killer searching for a place to dump his most recent victim. Fortunately God gives bears the sense to stay in their dens on stormy nights and I awoke soggy but unmolested. In the morning light I noticed some week-old bear spoor. In fact, some was stuck to my shoe.

I brought a cell phone on this trip. Before leaving, I checked the service area map and was pleased to find a solid green stripe down the pacific coast highway. However, someone in marketing must have asked his children to fill in the map with a green felt pen. Certainly the complaint department was not consulted. Anyway, they had their little joke on me. "No Service" was the usual result when I tried to call Kathyrn anywhere on the trip. But to be fair, I traveled mostly in places where people go to get away from phone calls.

I have a small rearview mirror that clips onto my glasses. It gives a great view of my left ear if it gets out of alignment but it lets me see who is menacing me from behind. I wish I had it when I was substitute teaching.

My bike has a bell on the handlebar. It gives a single clear "ding" when I flick the lever and it is a sound God can hear. I got in the habit of giving a thank-you ding when I felt good, or when I passed a special milestone, or when a cautious motorist saved my life.

Sept. 12 At Gray's Harbor I had a choice: pedal the long way around Aberdeen and Hoquiam through congested traffic or take the small walk-aboard ferry directly to Westport. For $8 I took the ferry on one of its last runs of the tourist season and watched the miles go by with my butt comfortably off the saddle. Westport is full of chainsaw carvings and seashell souvenirs. I should have sent you one of those clamshell ashtrays with googly eyes glued on them. Tourist tackiness aside, Westport is a real working fishing town, if the smell is any indicator.

Sept. 13 Tonight's dinner in camp, rice with mushroom sauce and canned chicken, would have been a most satisfactory meal except that I made it with lemonade from my water bottle. Piquant! Reminder: buy pink lemonade from now on so I will not mistake it for water.

I met Curt and Krista touring on their tandem bike. She sat recumbent in front. He was in a standard saddle behind. They had to travel with minimal equipment to get it loaded on one bike but they could make it fly down the road. I had been a long time in relative solitude while passing through sparsely inhabited country, so finding them compatible, we stopped at a café for a lunch I enjoyed greatly because of their good company.

When I speak of meeting someone on the highway I usually mean that they came zooming up behind me. If they were gregarious they would stop to talk. Throughout the trip I pootled along at 35 miles a day while everyone else made at least 50 miles a day. The fastest were disappointed if they couldn't score 70 miles. As a pleasing result I met almost everyone on the road.

My routine was to get up soon after daybreak, dawdle over coffee and oatmeal before packing up. If there were other bikers in camp I took time to talk with them. I was always the last one out of camp, usually after 9:30.

In the afternoon I would consult one of my maps to see where the next campground was and decide how much zip I had left in me. When I have driven this route in a car it seemed that I was passing a state park or grocery store every few minutes. But on a bike I had to study what lay ahead because it was easy to get caught with hours to go before reaching the next grocery store or campground.

Bike touring is unlike wilderness hiking. Backpackers are mindful of carrying lightweight food for the duration of the hike. I had the luxury of shopping daily for food and didn't have to keep the weight down. After breakfast in camp, I could ride a few hours before I started looking for "Granny's Café" or "Fat Freddy's Burger Barn", though often I scored no better than a mom and pop grocery store where the deli consisted of frozen burritos and a microwave.

I like my self-inflating air mattress, but if I let it inflate fully it's like trying to sleep on top of a large dog.

Just south of Raymond, I was hit by a heavy rain that took only ten seconds from first splat to tropical downpour, requiring a hurried search for shelter. Fifteen minutes later I resumed riding in a light sprinkle with a double rainbow for company. The next turn in my fortune was a paved, level bike path far enough from the highway to get away from the constant howl of tires and growl of engines. God gets another ding from my "Thanks, Lord" bell for that. But a headwind sprang up after the heavy rain, and slowed me down to waking pace. Pedaling against the wind was bad enough, but the reeking fish-meal plant upwind took my mind off such trifles. Is it too obvious to state that you can't hold your nose and ride a bicycle at the same time?

Somewhere in southwest Washington I saw an expensive house nearing completion at a forested riverfront site. The architect had given it some tasteful Colonial touches but the beauty was marred by the tall chain-link fence topped with coils of razor wire. I thought it suitable for a banana republic tyrant in exile. Who could be happy there?

My trip was planned to take advantage of the tailwinds of summer. So many touring cyclists go from north to south that the highway departments have made the shoulders wider in the southbound lane. If this rain will stop, fair weather will come in with the wind at my back.

The state parks on the west coast all had special "Hiker-Biker" camp sites for a reduced fee: $3 to $4 in Oregon and California and $10 in Washington, compared to more than $15 for anyone arriving in a motor vehicle. Of course I liked the nominal charge, but something that really made the trip special for me was meeting other cycle tourists clustered in the common campground. I was always interested to see who I would be sharing the camp with at the end of the day.

34

This afternoon, as I was examining the menu at a café, a gent at the counter casually commented "I hear the Monte Cristo sandwich is good." I ordered one. A few minutes later I heard one of the customers snicker. When I looked at the waitress she suppressed a smirk. An inside joke was being played on someone. Was it me? Did they have a Monte Cristo left over from yesterday? Was it notoriously overpriced? I asked the waitress to change my order. She laughed and told me that the joke had been on her; she had never made a Monte Cristo and didn't know how.

Sept. 14 My last day in Washington scored low on my fun meter. By mid afternoon I could see it was going to be a long ride to a campground. In the late afternoon rain I pushed on to the Columbia River where I intended to stay at a hostel on the Washington side. I arrived cold, wet, and tired to find that the hostel listed in my guidebook had ceased operation a few years ago. Three miles farther out of my way I found an RV camp. The proprietress said I could put up my tent under the picnic shelter for $20, but it proved to be shabby, windblown, and dark. I stalled for a better deal. "Ten dollars would suit me better", I offered. But she held to her price, so rather than be uncomfortable and overcharged I said, "No, thanks" and left, with little hope of finding another place to stay in such a small town. But five blocks down the street I found a cheerier looking sport fisherman's RV camp. The owner offered me a sheltered carport for $6. "Aw, Heck, make it $5" he said. He led me over to a carport by a large dining hall where he paused to regard my pathetic appearance. He then offered me the use of the hall itself, a neat well-lit room with tables and a galley. Alright! That's all it took to turn a dismal day into warm reception. Well, that and a big dinner, a hot shower, and a tall glass of scotch.

You know your trip is in trouble when you are consuming mosquito repellent faster than sunblock

Sept. 15 For three hundred miles I had been fretting about crossing the Columbia River Bridge at Astoria. It is notoriously long, narrow, shoulderless, steep, windy, and jammed with commercial traffic. My connections with the Almighty are thin at best, but in this case I seriously asked to be ferried across the waters in the palm of God's hand. The day I crossed the bridge, my care was delegated to one of His minor assistants who hadn't done this much before. I tried to ride on the roadway, but chickened out with the first passing dump truck, then walked my bike 4 miles, teetering on the narrow curb with my traffic-side elbow held in close to me. As bad as the Astoria bridge was, the bridge over Young's Bay south of town proved to be worse, with rush hour traffic and only an 8 inch wide curb to tiptoe on. I could not believe that the highway department had posted an "Oregon Bike Route" sign on that killer. The two bridges and a very challenging tunnel on the Washington side left me feeling frazzled and cowed as I cranked off the remaining showery miles to a hostel in Seaside, Oregon.

What had been an outdated motel is now a hostel ("youth" has been dropped from "youth hostel"). $17 got me access to a cozy common room, kitchen, laundry, internet terminal, and a small bedroom with 3 double bunks crowded into it. My roomies were two rain soaked motorcyclists who had draped their leather riding suits everywhere to dry. I would rather have shared the room with several large wet dogs but their conversation was good. Joachim, a German on a BMW (what else?) was on a journey to Tierra del Fuego. From him I learned that there is no continuous highway from North America to South America. Near Panama, in an area called the Darien Gap, there are only donkey trails and rivers without bridges. One must take an ocean-going ferry to Colombia or Peru. I also met Chris W., a solo cyclist riding the coast route for the third time. Though he rode farther than I each day, we still met several times down the road.

Sept. 16 I stayed tonight at Oswald West State Park. Cars must park near the highway but everyone hikes into the campground. Wheelbarrows are provided for car campers with lots of gear. A wheelbarrow load of rats is also provided, gratis. The bold little vermin were crowding me for space on the table before my dinner was ready. I batted a little one off my pant leg. By dark they were fearless. They opened up my pack during the night, ate all my oatmeal, had a noisy tussle with some raccoons, and left my panniers open to the rain.

Sept. 17 My tent had let me down for the last time. I shoved the plastic rain fly in the garbage and shipped the tent home in a wet wad for future use as a fair weather doghouse. My neighbors loaned me their top quality two person tent which I picked up, general delivery, at the Tillamook Post Office.

Sept. 18 I made camp at Cape Lookout State Park, one of Oregon's many long sandy beaches. My evening stroll on the beach was cut short by a brilliant flash of lightning and an immediate clap of thunder. My eyes were seeing blue jags and my ears were ringing as I hurried back to the tent. For the next 20 minutes the tent rattled as if a dump truck was unloading BB shot on it, but I was a dry guy in my new tent!

Sept. 18 Today was one of my shortest and wettest runs, twenty miles interrupted by downpours. I was ready to throw in the towel, if I could dry off with it first. When I arrived in tiny Pacific City I was ready to pay for a motel room. Unfortunately there was an overabundance of salmon fishermen in town and the streets were abuzz with a Vespa rider's rally. The only room available was a $125 suite. In a dismal funk I pedaled slowly out of town wondering what to do when I spotted the smallest county park I had ever seen. Otters glided by in the river 15 feet away. The $3 price was right and one of the sites was vacant. Problem solved. Give God a ding on the thank-you bell.

Sept. 19 I awakened to improving weather. The headwinds of the last 400 miles reversed overnight and clearer skies were coming. The tailwinds kicked in as I had hoped.

I made a lighthearted run to a state park situated right in the middle of Lincoln City, lighthearted except for missing the sign and going 4 extra miles before I got suspicious. I attribute that to being a little ditzy at the end of a long day.

By now I realized that as a package, my bike and I were ideally suited for 35 miles a day. Once I accepted this and did not push this limit life was sweet. I can look back and see that I stopped at more vista points and took more pictures early in the day. In the last weary hour of the day, if I saw a sign, "World Famous Lighthouse –1/4 mile" I would say, "Nah, too far." OK, maybe I'd go if they were going to blow it up in the next 20 minutes.

My campsite in Lincoln City was across the street from a residential neighborhood. With my new cell phone I could order a pizza! I regret that I did not pull this stunt off, but I had already begun a pot luck meal with some new-found friends, Margie and David.

Margie and David were just beginning their ride down the Oregon coast on a spectacular rig, a tandem bike pulling a one-wheeled "Bob" trailer. This was the human powered equivalent of Oregon's notorious triple trucks. We kept company with each other throughout a week, and delightful company they were. It was great to see familiar faces in camp each evening and discuss the sights of the day.

Sept. 20 My lunch stop at Boiler Bay Park under a sunny, blue sky was a "10" with a bonus of superior whale watching. Gray whales were rolling and diving among the kelp, close enough that I could see the white encrustations on their heads.

Sept. 20 This trip is on a roll. I found a supermarket where I could buy a large salmon fillet and some white wine for dinner. Via the cellular grapevine I learned that my young friend, Liz, and her friend Chris were nearby. I joined them at their camp for breakfast. Liz, the Nature Girl of her generation, is a gifted forager, among her talents. She made a hot breakfast with cooked apples gleaned from an abandoned orchard, huckleberries picked on yesterday's hike, and 47 other ingredients besides oatmeal.

If you put half a dozen cyclists together, the conversation will quickly turn to gearhead tech-talk. I was always the odd duck in these sessions. My big, heavy bike was a Basset among Greyhounds. My tires were the size of a salami when everyone else ran on Vienna sausages. I rode sitting upright like an old geezer with a bad back when everyone knows you're supposed to lean way down with underslung handlebars. The piece of my equipment that drew the most comment (much of it polite) were my homemade panniers. I used plastic file boxes from Wal-Mart for the front panniers and plastic wastepaper baskets for the rear set. They were as distinctly homemade as Davy Crockett's coonskin cap and every bit as classy, but they served me well for more than 1100 miles

I was passed today by two road-worn and leathery gents on bicycles. One called out "Hello from Czech Repooblik" as he sped by. They were in Brazil by dinner time.

Sept. 22 This morning's 3 mile push up a steep grade ended at a rocky headland shining in the morning sun. I savored the view while regaining my breath, then started down, reveling in the descent: the wind in my face, the music of chirping birds, and the scent of smoking brake pads in the late summer air. Glorious!

I have begun noticing shattered auto glass in many of the wayside parking areas. Take your valuables with you when you park in these places, or someone else will.

I have begun a two-part weight loss program. Every few days I mail home some items I can do without, and it has added up to a few pounds. Also, by Eureka I had lost 14 pounds of my own weight. My belt is on the last notch and is still loose.

Always the last one out of camp and last to arrive at day's end, I have begun to feel constrained by the shortening days. Reading by flashlight before bedtime is no great drain on the batteries though; three sentences in my book and ZZZZZZ...

I have named my bike: "Speedy". It can be said sarcastically when pushing the heavy bugger up Three Mile Grade, as in "Come on Speedy you can make it", or it can be said sincerely when rocketing down the other side of the mountain, as in "Whoa, Speedy. Don't come apart on me now!"

At a vista point turnout I noticed a bronze replica of a surveyor's tripod set up to look out over a grand view of the Pacific. It bore a plaque dedicated to the memory of a former county surveyor. The transit was missing. The message I took was that the good man had packed up his tools and gone home to rest.

Sept. 23 I have a sad tale to relate, a modern Grapes of Wrath. A couple in their late 30's were camped at the Sunset Beach hiker-biker site when I arrived. I will call them Belch and Naggy Loser. The Losers had been trying to drive across three states in a $50 car in hope that a friend could fix Belch up with a job. They had been car camping beside the road to save money and were asleep in their tent at a remote spot around midnight when they awoke to gunfire in the vicinity of their car 150 feet away. Belch jumped up and shouted, "Hey! We're campin' up here. Stop shootin!" He heard some voices, then door slams, and a car roared away. Thieves had broken into their car, stolen the few things of value, and shot out the windows and tires. After picking through the mess in the morning and hitching a ride to the state park, they were roosting in the $3/ night campsite until they could figure out their next move. The Sheriff had made his report and put them in contact with a reporter for the local newspaper. This was big news in a quiet county and the story made the front page. With luck someone might come to their aid, but for now Belch and Naggy were stuck with little to do but drink beer and fight with each other, at which they were well practiced. Mr. Loser liked to chug a 16 oz. Budweiser and signal his satisfaction with a virtuoso belch. He did it for the same reason the donkey brays; he liked the sound. Mrs. Loser spoke only to veto her husband's orders, as in "I ain't gonna wash none of your damn dishes." On my way out I slipped a few bucks under a six-pack on their table. If they hadn't awakened me in the middle of the night with a loud squabble I would have given more.

Sept. 24 I spent the day on a scenic alternate called Seven Devils Road. I suspect the seven devils were hills, but seventy was a more accurate number.

This evening 43 cyclists on fast road bikes swept into camp like a tsunami. They were on a van-supported and catered fund raising ride. On the road they carried little more than an energy bar and a credit card and were capable of 80 mile days. They were a wiry and lean lot. My Old Geezer line wouldn't go with this group though; there were a dozen men older than I. They talked as if an 80 mile day was nothing, but a strong whiff of Ben-Gay told a different story. But, Oh, the Spandex in shocking colors!

I met another solo touring cyclist, Peter W. who has gone most of the way around the U.S., though not all in one trip. His rides for a month, returns home to Florida for a while, then picks up where he left off for another month's ride when he can get the time.

Sept. 25 On the road by 8:15 this morning (much earlier than usual) with 48 miles to go to the next campground. Today is Kathyrn's birthday and I am missing her and feeling all of the 700 miles that separate us.

Another difficult bridge crossing at Rogue River, where I walked my bike across. I had been asking various cyclists about their tactics for dealing with dangerous bridges and narrow roads. Invariably they told me that they just "took the lane" and insisted on their right to a place on the roadway, expecting motorists to give them room. I got to feeling low and chicken-hearted about my habit of walking my bike through tight spots or waiting beside the road for traffic to clear. Then it struck me: all the cyclists I talked to were younger than 30 and still thought they were immortal, so I'm still with the chicken plan. I later heard that a couple crossing the Rogue bridge on a tandem had ridden on the roadway, holding up traffic and were given a horn blast by a logging truck. Scared, they wobbled and fell, skinning themselves and damaging the bike, but were otherwise unhurt.

Beer doesn't travel well by bicycle and I have been missing it. I had a rare bit of luck to find a well stocked store only two miles from camp today. Join me in a Foster's?

Sept. 27 I pedaled past Pelican Bay Prison. God, but they are vast and faceless concrete buildings. The sight made me feel particularly free. God gets another "ding" on my thank-you bell.

My guide book took two paragraphs to describe the dangerous hills south of Crescent City. There were the usual challenges of logging trucks and narrow roads, but with the added problem of coastal fog. A friend living nearby had taken this so seriously that he offered to put me and my bike in his pickup truck and drive me through. But when the time came I found an alternate route, a branch of the Pacific Coast Hiking trail with a free campsite along the way. I pitched my tent there late in the day. The camp is accessible only by bike or on foot and it was the only park I stayed in with a creek as the only source of water. Two other parties were camping there, or "homesteading" to use a sheriff's term for anyone camping long-term with no home to return to. A gray haired man, lean and tattooed and his Indian wife welcomed me with toothless smiles and an offer of some cowboy coffee boiling over the fire. A solo chap on a bicycle trip with an indeterminate end was the other occupant. He was on a tour of any free places he could find.

Sept. 28 Early this morning I began the climb out of camp on a hiking trail that led up a high cliff. The trail would have been too steep for a horse, hard work for a mule, and it was all this old geezer could do to push and pull his bike up that chute. Often I stopped to rest after progressing only 6 inches. There was over a mile of this. At the crest the trail changed to short ups and downs but was still too rocky and rooty to ride. A mile farther on, the path gradually leveled and widened until I could ride easily through the forest of giant redwoods on a carpet of moss and redwood needles. In places where the earth was bare I marveled at how much it resembled pavement, very much like pavement indeed. I had to scrape through the debris, and actually see the white line painted on the pavement before I realized that I was riding on an old stretch of the coast road. I had the forest and road all to myself as it wound through the misty redwoods far from the souvenir shops and the noise of highway traffic. Feeling very aware of my remote isolation in a forest gone back to wilderness, I thought of a new use for my thank-you bell: "Notice to bears, I'm coming through. Ding, Ding"

Fair weather continued for the ride to Prairie Creek State Park. At the ranger station I met Derek, a motorcyclist from England, and a Cockney I would guess from his accent. He had logged over 24,000 miles in North America and was about to head to Mexico. He asked me to watch for someone he wanted to rendezvous with. "She's a German woman named Tina, cycling solo. You won't miss her bright red panniers." Tell her I'm in site #41 and I'd really like to see her.

I had heard of Tina several hundred miles back. One of my camp mates had befriended her for a few days but eventually continued on by himself. The grapevine had been buzzing with news of Tina ever since.

At dusk a solo woman cyclist matching the description wheeled into camp. I said, "Hello, someone is looking for you. He said to keep an eye out for a lovely German lass." She blushed and gave a coy toss of her curls. "Oh, good, she said "Derek is here. It's his birthday and I've brought a cake strapped to my bike for 30 miles."

Sept. 29 As I was packing up to leave Prairie Creek I watched as a fellow standing in the adjacent camp gave a loud shout and fell to the ground. I raced a hundred feet to his side, trying to remember what to do. Check for vital signs? What vital signs? By the time I got there he was conscious and I asked if he was all right. "Oh, I'm fine", he said. "Really, I'm OK." I helped him to his feet and he said, "I'm a yogi. When I do this one exercise just right all this energy comes up through me in a big WHOOSH. Sometimes I fall down. Did I yell? Sometimes I do that without realizing it. I took him by the shoulders and in a teasing tone said "Or maybe you wanted to play a little joke and scare the bejeebers out of me! He grew quite serious and denied this several times. He explained how he had studied yoga and spiritual healing with many masters in India and other coun-

44

tries. With perfect sincerity he told me that one of his masters had been able to levitate himself. In his words: "I was chopping vegetables for the evening meal and my yoga master levitated up 10 or 12 feet, then drifted sideways 20 feet or so while he gave me some advice on how to proceed with the dinner preparations. Then he just settled back to earth"

He also told me about an incident that happened the night before I arrived. He had been leading a woman through some spiritual healing. I imagine it was a kind of regression therapy. The woman began reliving a very traumatic event in her childhood and screamed, "Stop! Go away! Don't!", all in a quiet and crowded state park. Several campers picked up their cell phones and called 911. When the sheriff arrived the woman was at first unwilling to come forward, putting my yogi acquaintance in an uncomfortable spot. But the woman eventually spoke up and all was settled an hour later.

Sept. 30 Patrick's Point State Park has the worst hiker-biker site I've encountered. A street light shines on it all night, It's nearly a mile away from the phone and showers , and construction equipment growled all day 50 feet away.

A fox visited the camp just at dark. It was hardly bigger than a cat but had a tail large enough for a wolf. It noisily rummaged through a huge stack of dry leaves near my tent far into the night.

One of my little myths evaporated today. I had hoped to go to the plaza in Arcata, my old college town, and just hang out with some of today's students. Perhaps I would spot my younger self there, or at least some Humboldt Honeys. I didn't expect to find Frat Boys and Betty Co-ed, but I was disappointed to find dozens of panhandling, spaced out, dreadlocked street people. They were very, very late for class. One lay like a beached sea lion shaded by his cardboard sign that read "Please Help." Help him do what?, I wondered. He isn't doing anything.

Oct. 1-3 Eureka, my home town. I stayed 3 days visiting family and friends. This was the first time I had stayed anywhere more than one night. My mother had been worried that I would show up ragged and dirty. She was ready to hose me off on the patio and buy me new clothes. The truth was that I was pretty spiffy if you overlooked a little chain grease on my socks.

Oct. 5 Richardson Grove, a very popular state park, was all but vacant. Though the weather was perfect it was late in the camping season. I was losing minutes of daylight each week.

Oct. 6 For 50 miles I had been worrying about an area of dangerous road north of Leggett. One side of the narrow road is a sheer rock face, scarred by many trucks that had dodged a collision. The other side is a guard rail pinned to a dropoff into the river canyon. The whole area is a series of blind curves. I pedaled up to the worst of these and stopped a long time watching the traffic and gaging my chances of making it through. I saw that, once committed, there was a 30 second period when luck was my only protection. I took a picture of the trouble spot, hoping that someone sorting through the wreckage later wouldn't find this as the last image on my crumpled camera. I waited until there was no traffic in sight and started through.

I drew an unlucky card. At the worst possible moment a semi came flying up behind me. I could hear him braking and grabbing gears. I moved out toward the middle of my lane and gave a signal for him to stay behind me. Damn it! Instead, he accelerated and tried to go around me, into the oncoming lane. Another semi appeared at exactly the wrong moment, hurtling toward us around the curve. The oncoming driver stood on his brakes so hard that I could hardly see his wheels for all the blue smoke boiling up. The two trucks finally stopped 40 feet apart with one very shaky bicyclist in the middle. All parties were too unnerved to do any shouting or finger waving, so I just pedaled to the nearest turnout to give my adrenalin glands a rest.

That sunny "I'm so glad to be alive" feeling is really quite different than "I'm glad they haven't been able to kill me yet"

Note to Caltrans: Please install a flashing light marked "Bicyclists on Roadway" at the ends of this zone with a push button that cyclists can operate. Better yet, make that a barrier gate like railroad crossings have.

I met another "homesteader" at a state park. He had an entire section of the park to himself. I attribute this to the 5 wolf-dogs he had staked out around his camp.

Near Myers Flat I met a cyclist pulling a trailer with a large flag that read "Jesus Saves." I wanted to ask him which was greater: the spiritual tailwind he got from his flag or the aerodynamic drag. I guess it depends on whether your destination is Heaven or Myers Flat.

I met another cyclist with a longer, grayer beard than mine. He was on an art journey and carried an easel, canvasses and paint.

I met a third cyclist, pulling a trailer with a surfboard on it. He was heading inland. I think I'm getting into a special California Culture zone.

I left highway 101 at the town of Leggett and got on to Highway 1 for the rest of my trip. But first there was the Legget hill to climb. At 2000 feet it is the highest point on the coast route, 7 % grade much of the way, and mostly hairpin switchbacks. My guidebook says that the roadside is dotted with discarded panniers and the bleached bones of cyclists who did not "make the grade". I topped up my water bottles and spent several hours walking and pushing my bike, wishing the crest would come into view.

As soon as I got onto Highway One I started seeing "wanted" posters for the person who killed a young couple near Jenner. They were found shot to death in their sleeping bags where they had camped overnight at a remote beach. I checked several sources to find if they had committed any reckless act that would put them at risk, but it seemed to be a random killing requiring only a deranged murderer and an opportunity.

I have been horn honked, fingered, and dog barked, but those memories evaporated when some girls drove by and shouted "We love you." They may have actually shouted "Move it Gramps," but my hearing isn't what it used to be.

Oct. 8 I have left the Pacific Northwest behind. I spotted my first City People in the town of Mendocino: Women with little hair and tiny eyeglasses. Men who selected the clothing they would wear that day today with some thought beyond 'what's on top of the pile.' (They were likely to choose a drapey black jacket and Birkenstocks). Remember, I have come through a thousand miles of logging town culture where Guns & Ammo magazine outsells Vogue. From Mendocino southward German- made roadsters outnumbered pickup trucks. I see the point of the town's nickname, Spendocino.

The redwood forests are behind me now, exchanged for the grassy hills and eucalyptus lined lanes of the Mendocino coast. Every few miles a creek has cut a gully into the land and the narrow road dives down to a modest bridge and winds back up to the grasslands again.

I'm loving the fair weather. The tailwinds are strong enough to carry me up a slight incline.

Oct. 10   Please sit down now because I'm going to unload my condor story. I saw a California Condor today, about a mile south of Timber Cove, perched on a rocky promontory over the ocean. It was all black and about 34 inches from head to rump with tail feathers sticking out beyond that. Before I could get my camera ready it unfolded its wings and launched off the rock, dropping out of sight in an instant. I saw it at a distance of 400 feet. Now that I have checked several bird books I would say that it was a juvenile, though the same books do not admit to the existence of condors north of Big Sur. The only evidence that runs counter to my claim is that all known condors are prominently marked with numbers on the underside of their wings. I did not see numbers or bright paint. Was it a South American Condor out of his usual range in this El Niño year? I don't know. Was it the world's largest turkey vulture? It's like sighting Bigfoot. If you discovered later that it was really a 10 foot tall human being wouldn't you say that was pretty extraordinary too?

I was getting close to the end of my ride. I had intended to make it to San Francisco, but the route was about to turn inland through satellite towns and suburbs. Besides, I was having a hard time contending with the Sunday night traffic returning to the Bay area. I decided to end my ride at Bodega Dunes State Park. My odometer showed 1150 miles

I spent the next 5 days visiting family and luxuriating in homes with electric light, real beds and refrigeration. I put my bike on Amtrak and rode back in 24 hours the distance it had taken me 31 days to pedal.

I liked Amtrak. The staff was great, the $68 ticket was a bargain and security checks were nil. Kathyrn met me in Seattle.

She loved standing out on the platform, watching the big locomotive roll in with a hiss of brakes and being able to give me a hug when I stepped off the train. Try that at the airport!

I will close with an incident that occurred in the last minutes of my ride. Somewhere up in Oregon I had heard about a young couple cycle touring with their 2 year old daughter in a baby trailer. I thought this was amazing and I wanted to meet them, but always I heard that they were just a day ahead or behind. At Bodega Dunes, a couple with a baby in a trailer wheeled into camp. It was them! I thought I would wait a few minutes for them to get settled before going over to meet and congratulate them. But they came over straightaway, looked at me and my bike, and said, "You must be the "Neal" we have been hearing about for the last 700 miles!

That's my story and I'm stickin' to it.

Neal
Copyright Neal Fridley 2004

The Fridleys go west

My grandpa, Harry Benjamin Fridley, was born in 1888, the year of three eights, as he said. He was born into a world that would be strange to us. In 1888 Henry Ford rode a horse into town when he needed something. The automobile was still a few years away. No one flew here and there. The Wright brothers thought they had a bright future ahead of them, building bicycles.

Harry Fridley married Helen Holgate at the start of WWI when he was 26. I'm almost sure I was 26 once.

The newlyweds had 160 acres of dry wheat farm in Montana, not far from Yellowstone.

There was an irrigation ditch on the farm which the kids played in (more like lived in) all summer, but household water was brought in on a horse drawn wagon. My Dad said there wasn't a single tree in sight. No Wonder Montana's State Tree is the telephone pole.

Harry and Helen had seven kids: Ben, Warren, Bob, Dig, Rosa Mae, Isla, and Eleanor.

In 1928 times weren't too hard for most folks, but the Fridleys had a couple of years when crops were poor and they needed this year to be good if they were going to hang on.

The wheat came on real good and it looked like the year would pay.

In July a summer storm filled the sky with black clouds and the hail began to fall. It cut those wheat stalks right down to the ground and Grandpa stood at the window and cried, the only time the kids had seen him cry.

Kathyrn calls it one of God's terrible blessings. At first it looks like you've hit rock bottom, but you go on and later it turns out all right.

They sold out the farm and bought a new Ford touring car. Harry and Helen and the seven kids made a mighty heavy load.

Ben and Warren and Bob and Dig Rosa Mae and Isla and sitting on Grandma's lap was little baby Eleanor. She goes by Macy now. Maybe she just wasn't the Eleanor type.

They left behind their farm and home and family and friends. Grandpa felt real bad about leaving their dog, Zip, behind. He often said we could have made room for Zip somewhere. We could have made room for Zip.

They turned their faces west and rolled away in a cloud of Montana dust, and some of that Montana dust is stickin' to 'em still.

They stayed in tourist camps along the way. Kinda like K.O.A., only with outhouses and no place to plug in your hair curlers and TV.

They rolled on through Montana, Idaho, Oregon, and into California, a route so many more families would follow in the hard depression years ahead.

There's a song that goes "California is a Garden of Eden. A wonder to live in or see. But believe it or not you won't think it's so hot if you ain't got the Do Re Mi."

They were going to a place where it was always warm and

sunshiny: California. Well, Eureka anyway. That's an inside joke to my family.

Somewhere around Crescent City they saw the Pacific Ocean. My father tried to look clear across it. Maybe see China.. The kids waded in the ocean too! Hot Diggity Dog! My uncle Clarence favored that expression as a boy and it stuck to him as his nickname all his life.

They reached their destination, Eureka, up on the Northern California coast, my hometown. I always thought Eureka was filled with people who settled there because they ran out of gas money and couldn't get to anywhere better. But it wasn't that way for the Fridleys. Harry had a sister in Eureka. She helped them settle in. He got a job at the Eureka Woolen Mill for thirty five cents an hour. Don't knock it; work ten hour days; it adds up.

They had indoor plumbing and store-bought bread and an old sow and a milk cow too. Oh, that store-bought bread. Not like that old home-made stuff.

We lost Uncle Dig in World War II when his bomber didn't make it back to the base in the Aleutians. All the family wondered what became of him. Was he shot down and taken prisoner? Does he lie at the bottom of the sea ? The Navy gave Grandma and Grampa a gold star to hang in the window when Dig didn't come home. Too many gold stars hanging in too many windows in those years. And now 50 years later the truth is known. In 1998 the wreckage of his plane was found on the side of a volcano in Kamchatka, eastern Russia.

Gramp's children grew up and got married. The six Fridley kids all went in together to build a little home for grandma and grandpa to have for their own. That's when I was old enough to know them.

At a family gathering in my folks backyard, Grandma Fridley showed us how to call hogs: SOOOOO-EEEEEEE PIG, PIG, PIG PIG SOOOO-EEEEEEE. I believe Hogs clear back in Montana perked up their ears and headed west. Her voice did carry. She never did show how she called the kids in to dinner.

Grandpa let me have my first sip of beer and showed me how to roll a cigarette. Crease that Wheat Straw paper and hold it like this. Tap your pouch of Bull Durham Tobacco over the paper 'til you got a nice, even load.   Atta Boy. Pretty soon you'll be able to roll a cigarette with one hand, riding on a bucking bronco at midnight in a hurricane.

We lost Grandma in 1959 and Grandpa in '69 and now those seven kids number but a few. But their children and grandchildren make a big happy crowd, about 80 or so. They never will sit still long enough for me to count 'em

So that's my story about Grampa and Grandma, and I just want to say "pass your family story on too".

Delivering "Sans Souci"

My longtime friend Rip Knot had been working a deal for more than a year to be the delivery skipper on a new 65' blue water power yacht called Sans Souci (French for "out of Sushi"). Rip recently got his captain's 100 ton license and was preparing to take the boat from Seattle to France. Months ago, when I heard about the trip, I said "sign me up", and when the time came to pick a crew I was available for the first leg of the trip, to Dana Point, California. Hold the phone... this just in: Sans Souci means "without a care"

The Crew:

Captain: Rip Knot: Ballard waterfront character, shipwright, with many yacht deliveries in his log.

Engineer: Ric Holl (Aussie): Lifelong yachtie, eight years experience as paid skipper on private sailing yachts all around the world.

Cook: Tiffany Clark: Recently graduated college (B.A., philosophy), most recently a boatyard laborer, but cute and enthusiastic enough to get the job.

Bosun: Tiel Riis: a serious, very capable, and taciturn young man. His father owned the boatyard where the commissioning of the boat was done, but he earned his berth with his own abilities.

Mate: Neal Fridley: Loose Cannon, Dark Horse, drifty aging hippie; take your pick..

I joined the boat at her berth in Lake Union, Seattle on

Friday and spent the day shopping and stowing gear and provisions. When we went shopping for bedding at Sears,. Rip and I were totally out of our league. Sears is set up for women to come in and buy linens and frou-frou. Two guys who want sheets for odd shaped berths might as well be from Mars. We hit our stride down at the Sears tool department, though, with our order for "one or two of everything"

Young Tiffany was struggling with her new role as cook and provisioner. Her habit of living on granola and spring water had not prepared her for catering to four men who like greasy, fried breakfasts and meat and potatoes as often as possible. When asked how the provisioning had gone she proudly held up a small shopping bag of meat and a single bag of coffee. Rip grabbed his car keys and went shopping to avert a calamity.

By tradition or superstition, no one in Ballard starts a voyage on Friday. I once worked overtime around the clock outfitting a fishing ship that was badly overdue to leave for a season opening. She could have left on a Friday, but at a cost of tens of thousands of dollars, the captain contrived to leave on Saturday. Sans Souci also left on Saturday.

The fuel dock was only open half a day on Saturday. We had to run two, and later three big fuel nozzles to take on 1500 gallons of diesel in three hours so the fuel dock crew could go home.

When we transited the Ballard locks, the usual large crowd was there to gawk. We tried to look blase, but we were wagging our tails like big dogs allowed to ride in the back of a pickup truck.. Several spectators fired questions at us. "Where were we going?" We couldn't say "France" without smirking , so we said "San Diego". I Introduced myself to one family as Joe Bob Gates, Billy Gates' brother.

The engineer worked out a watch schedule, an ingenious one, really, that gave us three hours on during hours of darkness and four hour watches in daylight, and an equal amount of time off, yet no one got stuck with all nighttime duty. An experienced crewman was usually paired with a less experienced person on watch.

The owner was not aboard, so Rip got the Master's stateroom and the crew all had good guest staterooms. Teak everywhere you looked, marble vanities, private shower and head. The engine had been installed with great care to reduce noise and vibration, so I bunked down in the Straits of Juan de Fuca for a few quiet hours of sleep before my first watch.

At 0300 I joined Tiffany, my watch partner, in the pilothouse. We were still in the Straits, but now in zero visibility fog and an increasing swell. By the end of my watch I had gotten my sea legs.

The owner had retained a personal Weather Router, an expert you can call up to discuss your concerns about the weather ahead. We did this, as did several other large-yacht captains we spoke with. The consensus was 'stinky weather ahead'. Not the Perfect Storm, but sloppy going in 10-12 foot seas and 25 knot winds. We ducked in at Westport, WA for a day and a little later at Newport, OR to wait for an improvement. Cape Blanco and Cape Mendocino are nasty more often than not and this September was no exception. In 100 foot visibility, the Coast Guard escorted us in to Newport harbor where we tied up in the lee of the Rogue Ale Brewery. (Tasting room and pub open at 10:00 a.m.)

After two days, with a better forecast, we headed south again into 8-10 foot seas and 20 knots of wind. The boat had a very powerful dynamic stabilizer system, a pair of hydraulically operated fins mounted down at the turn of the bilge, very much like the pectoral fins of a whale. They got a real workout, as did the autopilot. Actually, the autopilot couldn't handle the sea state and we had to steer manually for a hundred miles, definitely something you had to get a feel for at night.

Off Cape Mendocino we heard a somewhat scared sounding woman on the VHF. Her message wasn't a mayday, but more a plea for ships in the area not to run over her in the fog. She was on a 27' sailboat with no wind, engine out, and no radar.

The area between San Francisco and the Farallones gave us the best show of marine life. Humpback whales came close enough for us to see their knobbly snouts. When their tail goes up, snap a picture quickly; you won't see them again. 6 foot white sharks swam lazily on the surface. Dolphins came by to play as well as sea lions and seals.

Our next sight of land was the barren, eroded landscape of southern California, Point Conception and the many oil rigs along the coast. The traffic intensified in the Santa Barbara channel, requiring three of us on watch. Our boat was equipped with an infrared television camera. At night we could see ships passing close by, the ghostly white glow of a crewman's body heat as he stood on deck, the white hot engine room, and the drifting plume of exhaust from the smokestack.

The Coast Guard came on the radio to announce that a ship near Catalina had reported a loud boom at the bow and a flash of light nearby in the darkness and then a cry for help at the ship's side. All vessels in the area were asked to keep watch for debris or survivors. We never heard any more about this collision at sea.

We tied up for good at Dana Point Marina and cleaned up the boat. I gathered up a handful of granular salt by wiping it off the cap rail.

While knocking around the nearby town I met a young man sitting in the shade of a palm tree by a bus station. All he had in the world was a second hand issue of Surf magazine and a grotesque mask about three feet long, a face painted on a palm branch. He cadged a free ride from the bus driver and boarded with me. When we I got off the bus, I had the mask and he had some of my money. I don't know how this happened. The mask is named OogaBooga. My wife declined it as a birthday present.

Homeboy makes a few observations about Southern California:

Don't bother looking for Latte/espresso stands at every corner. Liquor stores occupy those spaces.

In Seattle, a high priced marina complex like Dana Point would have one or two bookstores. Bring your own books from home if you want to read down here.

Laguna Beach, the next town north, has 30 highfalutin' art galleries, but any of you low faluters looking for a head gasket for your Volkswagen are S.O.L.

Laguna Beach has the usual number of pay phones, but they go unused. Use your cell phone.

Waterfront houses are packed together as tightly as possible, allowing exactly 24 inches of clear space between them, like people in an elevator standing without touching or talking.

I saw people wade right out into the ocean and they did not die of hypothermia. Swear to God.

All of the old beater cars have migrated to rural areas. Port Angeles must be their burying ground.

Later in the year others will take the boat through the Panama Canal and on to Nice, France. The owner is there now shopping for a permanent slip. If you have one to sell, let me know.

That's pretty much the yachting report for now,

Your Pal,

Neal

Seattle Drumfest

Dear Friends

Friday night, the opening ceremony, focuses on the spiritual side of drumming. Hundreds of attendees gather in a circle in a large hall. Chief Soggy Beaver of the Bellevue Tribe comes out and asks a blessing of the Great Spirit accompanied with chanting and beating his round frame drum.

Sister Starshine Lovechild takes over when the Beav is done. Her sermon is not much different, but the buzz words are New Age.

Third at bat is an African man named Esse. He is another story. I think he's straight up. I get the impression that he did not take up his religion as an alternative to getting a job after college, but was raised to it by his shaman father in Africa. Without much talk he gets down to the business of sanctifying the circle and clearing the air of any tainted spirit the crowd may have brought in. He has drawn a large circle on the floor and insists that no one intrude any part of their body into it, otherwise the ritual must stop and a correcting ritual performed. The tools of his trade include a goat hoof rattle, flywhisk and a bottle of Perrier. He takes a sip of water and sprays it noisily into the air. I noticed that the area where I was seated needed several applications of juju before he felt everyone's aura was spit-shined properly.

After Esse's bit, four symbolic arches are set up on the cardinal points of the circle and dancers perform a wooga-wooga liturgical dance. A conga line of nubile and not-so-nubile women from Orcas Island perform a lock-step caterpillar dance. They then curled up into cocoons and emerged as butterflies with silk sari-cloth wings and fluttered out through the North Arch. Over he next 45 minutes, the other points of the compass are similarly honored (the West is saluted by a troupe of Hawaiian dancers). The scheduled part of the ceremony culminates with all the dancers entering the circle to drum and dance. One by one, members of the congregation feel the call to join the inner circle, much like the braver sinners do at a tent revival. Finally, all of the spectators are invited to join in and the festival is declared open.

Saturday and Sunday offer workshops in every conceivable form of hand drumming. Irish, Native American, African, and Latin American, Drumming for spiritual ecstasy and Samba music. Conspicuous by their absence are the rock drumsets from modern western music. There is also a craft market and drop-in drum jams, but the focus of the weekend comes Saturday night.

Saturday night is the Drum Circle. The last year I went there were about 400 seekers, drums in hand, gathered around the large oval space. The leader/presenter/ringmaster is Arthur Hull, well known in the drum culture for the energy he can summon from a crowd of strangers. Arthur, like many leaders, is a mixture of windbag and sincere devotee. Except for his cotton drawstring trousers and African pillbox hat, he could pass for a Metro bus driver.

Motioning with his arms, he picks a segment of the circle and gives them a simple rhythm: Doom Taka Taka, and starts them going on that. Another group is assigned Taka Doom, Taka Doom on the counterpoint. Shakers, rattles and gongs all get their parts, and with a minimum of fuss and effort, 400 people are making that magic that gets your heart pumping and your butt shaking.

For now, that's the Fridley report on the drum festival.

Neal   September 2002

Rebert, Tweeter, and Egil

This story has been handed down from one generation to the next and the next. So, unless you figure out how to hand it back, you're stuck with it

It's about a bullfrog and some friends he met and it's about how music got started.

The frog's name was Rebert. When he went for a tasty fly and missed, he said "Yummy". When he hopped a long hop and landed hard on his butt, he said "Dammit". Nearly everything he said sounded like "Rebert", including his name.

When the moon came up and the stars came out he liked to sing them a song. Of course you know how the song went. All frogs still like to sing it.

One year, late in summer, the pond where Rebert lived began to dry up. When the pond got so small he couldn't wet all his toes at once, he decided it was a good time to go see the wide world. Off he went, hopping along through the forest in high spirits, croaking a song like we all do at the start of a journey.

He hadn't hopped so very far when a little bird called down from high in a tree. The bird's name was Tweeter. The bird said hello and asked Rebert where he was going and they discussed the weather but to you and me it would have sounded like tweet-er-weeter twee eeter. Rebert, Rebert, Rebert.

If Tweeter was supposed to be doing anything that day, he completely forgot about it, and in no time he was walking along beside Rebert just as if he had been invited along.

Tweeter knew hundreds of songs, and, since Rebert seemed to enjoy them, Tweeter tried to teach him a few. But when Rebert sang, it sounded, well, kind of froggy. Tweeter thought if the frog could play an instrument, their music would sound a lot better, so he plucked a blade of grass and showed Rebert how to hold it and blow through it to play a tune.

The two walked and chirped and croaked and kazooed as the miles went easily by. At the end of every chorus, Rebert would make a long leap and come down too hard on his butt and shout "Dammit", until Tweeter asked him to stop it.

At last they came to a babbling brook. It bibbled and babbled and tumbled and splished and splashed and it said "Hello and Fine day isn't it. Don't get many visitors here. Where are you going? Where did you come from?. Unusual to see a bird and a frog out for a walk. Fine day isn't it? Oh, did I already say that? Don't mind me, I have been known to babble on and on and…

Rebert said "hello to you too." His feet were hot and tired so he asked the brook if he could soak them a little. Sure said the brook. Would your bird friend like a bath? I don't mind a bit.

Rebert went for a swim and Tweeter had a bath and by the time they were done and dried off the brook had quieted down some and they began to get along very well. Tweeter and Rebert even asked the brook to go along with them. "I'd love to go", said the brook, "but I have to warn you that I can only go down-hill."

Well! That was no problem. Tweeter didn't care whether the way was uphill or down, but Rebert was delighted. The three of them walked and flitted and splashed along telling stories and singing songs to help the miles go by.

They passed out of the shady forest and came to a vast, sandy desert. It was hot and hard going for all of them, especially for the brook. Sometimes the sand was so deep the brook would sink completely out of sight. It was a struggle for Tweeter and Rebert to pull him out.

After many miles, Tweeter's sharp eyes spotted something white in the far distance. "It looks like bones", said Tweeter as they drew closer. And sure enough it was; the skeleton of a dead horse lying on its side in the sand

They were all surprised when the skeleton lifted up its head and gave them a rather bony hollow stare. "Is that really a brook out here in the desert?" the skeleton asked. "I could sure use a drink. I've been mighty dry these last twenty years. The horse stood up and shook himself, making quite a rattle, then introduced himself as Egil. The way he said it, though, it sounded like a neigh and a whinny. With the brook's permission, Egil drank and drank and drank. None of the travelers could believe how much he drank. Of course all the water drained out through his empty ribs, but Rebert and Tweeter and the brook thought it would be impolite to mention it. After he finished drinking, Egil noticed Rebert's grass-blade kazoo. "Is that grass? Real, green grass?" he asked. "I'm dying for a taste of grass" Don't you look at my blade of grass in that starved way! It's my kazoo. But when Rebert wasn't looking, Egil snitched it anyway and with his big teeth loose in their bony jaw sockets, he ate it. When the blade of grass dropped through Egil's rib cage, Tweeter picked it up and gave it back to Rebert, who kept a closer watch on it after that.

After his meal, Egil said he felt much refreshed and he would be happy to join them on their journey. So off they went singing a marching tune. Egil enjoyed the song and said he'd like join in, but all he could do was rattle his bones. They rattled a lot when he walked, but it was even worse when he galloped.

Rebert was getting very tired of walking in the desert and it seemed like they were going so slowly. He tried counting his steps and guessing how long it would take to get from one dune to the next. "Doesn't it seem like we are moving very slowly?" he asked. Tweeter said "yes that's been worrying me too"

"It's slow sand!" said Egil. Sure enough, they had stumbled into the dreadful slow sand.

"Don't try to speed up. It only makes it worse, Just keep going no matter how slow it seems. That's the only way out. So they plodded along till they could hardly stand it anymore. Rebert thought he was getting a blister. But they eventually got out.

After another day of travel the desert opened on to a grassy plain as far as they could see. Still farther on, Tweeter saw a tiny black object in the distance. As they got closer they could see it was black tent, round with a conical roof. A wisp of smoke curled up from a hole in the roof. "Is it on fire?" Rebert asked.

A man with a hunting bow appeared from behind the tent. He was as surprised to see the travelers as they were to see him. He said "My name is Jengiz and if you are hungry, please join me for dinner. I have just killed a fine fat marmot." He held up a little creature skewered with an arrow.

"No, thank you. We just ate a few days ago and we are not hungry right now. Really." Tweeter said. Egil kept on eating grass, which fell right back on the ground again, some of which he ate again, but he didn't seem to mind.

The brook said if it was all the same to the others, it would like to trickle over to a low spot and rest quietly. Rebert went to join the brook where he could soak his tired feet.

After Jengiz finished his marmot-on-a-stick dinner and they all had a nap, they gathered around a campfire in front of the tent. Jengiz asked if anyone knew any songs or good stories. Of course Tweeter and Rebert jumped right in with a song they had been practicing since they left the desert, but Egil just moped at the edge of the shadows. "Come, join in," Jengiz said to Egil, I'm just getting the hang of the chorus myself. Egil half-heartedly rattled a few of his ribs in time to the song.

Jengiz thought for a moment, then said "Horse, you old skeleton, I believe you have a few long hairs of your tail clinging to your skinny tailbone. May I have two of them?"

"Go ahead, I'm not particularly attached to them," Egil said. And he was right. The hairs came away with hardly a tug. Jengiz stretched the hairs across Egil's hollow skull and tied them in place.

"Listen to this," Jengiz said, and he gave the hairs a sharp twang. Amazing! What a beautiful tone! Twing, Twang, Twoing. No one was more amazed than Egil. He couldn't believe he was making such beautiful music. He was very proud and stood up tall and pranced around. "Do it again. Do it again," he neighed, putting his skull down where Tweeter and Rebert could reach. They all took turns playing favorite songs and making up new ones on the new instrument.

Then Jengiz picked up his hunting bow and drew it over the strings and made the instrument sing in a new way. He sang a sad song about his lonely life on the prairie. After he finished they all stared quietly into the firelight. But each knew in his own mind that they had found a fine new home.

You've probably wondered how music got started and now you know.

Harald and Sonia

I saw my old pals, Harald and Sonia, the King and Queen of
Norway, on TV the other day. A few years ago I had gone to see
them dedicate a mural in tiny Bergen Place park in Ballard, USA

It was a suitably drizzly day to welcome our guests. All the
Sons of Norway in their lodge meeting best clothes had packed
themselves around the podium to wait for the arrival, with the
rest of us foreigners at the fringes. A dozen Save the Whales
protesters also showed up carrying signs and holding on to large
helium filled mylar whale balloons. The streaks of blood they
had painted on the whales turned runny in the damp weather
and dripped on to the signs and protesters, but I think they were
happy with that.

The Norwegians were proud and pleased that their royal
family would visit their remote outpost, and generally wished the
protesters would go protest something in Antarctica.

I spotted a few familiar faces on the stage, the president of
the First Viking Bank, the founder of the Trawler/Processor As-
sociation, and Sig Erikson, my former employer and grand Uffda
of the Sons of Norway Lodge. They stopped fidgeting and
braced up when the sirens of the motorcade could be heard.

I was expecting ermine robes and crowns, or at least a sash
and tiara, but the K & Q stepped out of the limo in their civvies,
though the Queen wore a mink coat some of the ladies would
have mugged her for, had they met in an alley.

As the royal couple took their places, someone led the
crowd in singing the Norwegian National Anthem. A surprisingly
large number sang all the verses in Norwegian, and sang it well

and loud. I don't speak the language, but you can bet your last Króner that there was something in there about sparkling fjords and lofty forests; it was that kind of music

A group of protesters had showed up, ticked off at Norway's stance on whaling. One, a panda bear of a young man had a whale-shaped mylar balloon filled with helium. A heckler slipped up behind him, opened up his pocket knife, and popped the balloon. The protester, thinking to cause some panic, called out, "He's got a knife!", but he misjudged the audience. Norwegians are not an excitable group. When someone replied, "So what?", the protester gathered up his balloon debris and slunk away.

Eulogy For a Much Loved Cat

Our seventeen year old cat, Harley, has left us. On Friday the 13th of May he had a seizure that left him semi-conscious and unable to walk. Kathyrn and our friend Elaine took him to a vet and sent him on his way. We buried him with honor beneath a cherry tree in our orchard.

He had been losing ground this last year, dropping weight, getting stiff in his creaky old joints, and at last going entirely blind. When people go blind they can feel their way around with their hands or a cane. When Harley lost his sight he had to discover every obstacle with his tender nose. Still, he could navigate from room to room pretty well from memory, only occasionally getting lost in an open closet. I was surprised that he would still volunteer to go outside. So many unpredictable and troublesome things await a blind cat. I call it bravery, one of his lifelong traits.

When he could see, Harley looked at me with the most knowing eyes. Samba, our other cat, looks at me with her round, wide-awake eyes and I sense that the Lights Are On But Nobody Is Home. Harley's look always implied that he had something thoughtful to say and maybe someday he would tell you what it was.

Friends have asked how Harley got his name. Probably it was his Boss Cat attitude or his uneven purr. Maybe it was because he was the noisiest cat I've ever known. He liked to howl for the same reasons lions roar.

He was a cat to stand his ground rather than run and hide.

I admired this in him unless he was underfoot on the stairway or unwilling to yield the sofa. This territorial boldness was the cause of much conflict between us in our early years together. We lived on our sailboat Orion then, and choice spaces to sit were few. We fought little turf wars daily, but eventually signed a truce when I compromised by picking him up and holding him whenever I sat in his favorite spot. He was always ready to lay at full length on me when I was on the couch. He did not have that aloofness usual to cats.

He used up at least one of his lives when we lived on our boat. We were very careful to keep him from roaming free at dockside, but one day he escaped and I saw him poised on the cap rail, ready to spring onto the neighboring boat. His leap fell short and he splashed into Shilshole Bay. Kathyrn rushed up from below and may have actually said "Save my baby!" I picked up a ten foot boat pole and ran down our dock and around to the other boat to rescue him, but the pole hung up on some rigging cables and snapped in half in my hands. I stood there, brainless, trying to comprehend what had happened. Kathyrn surely must have wondered when the other two Stooges would show up to help. In the meantime, Harley had been cat-paddling back and forth between the two sheer walls of the boat hulls. Kathryn wasted no time in jumping into the bay, fully clothed. Harley, of course, seized onto her arm with every available claw as Kathyrn held him up out of the water, though she could do little but tread water herself. By this time I had regained some sense and went to a space at the head of the slip where I could reach the water. Kathyrn shook Harley so hard that he lost his grip and she threw him fifteen feet toward me. I thought twice about reaching down to him and all those desperate claws, but no matter, he latched on to the wooden pier and hauled himself out of the bay and ran straightaway into the boat cabin to hide. Kathyrn swam to the pier and I helped her, with considerable struggle, onto the dock. The story could end there, but our troubles were not over.

Kathyrn's glasses were at the bottom of the harbor, and I would spend an hour in a wet suit and mask recovering them. And Harley needed comforting. After his dip in the bay, he had scatted into the cabin and crawled under the covers of MY SIDE OF THE BED, the little knothead! The bedding would need a trip to the laundry. I picked Harley up, undecided whether to hug him or strangle him, and set him out on the dock to hose the saltwater out of his fur. Oy! The howling and caterwauling! A passer-by glared at me with disgust at my cruelty.

Harley was no sea-cat. Whenever I started Orion's engine he hid in my sock drawer and could not be coaxed out until the anchor was down and the engine was quiet. Living on a boat is about the unhandiest life imaginable and a cat's litter box made it even worse. I got it into my head to train him to use the boat's head (toilet) with a contraption called Kitty Whiz. It was a cat litter pan that fit into the toilet bowl. The idea was that once he got started using it, a hole in the center of the pan could be gradually enlarged until the pan could be taken out altogether. Harley put up with this for about a week and then let me know he'd had enough. He stopped using the Kitty Whiz. But where was he going? After a few days I sniffed out the answer: the sail locker. He used our $2000 spinnaker for a cat box. A spinnaker is a challenging, even terrifying sail to put up at best and now we found even more reason to leave it alone.

Here in Port Angeles, sometimes Harley would take a notion to go walkabout to visit the cats next door. Even though he was separated from the neighbor cats by a wire screen, their company had a powerful effect on him, changing his character completely. The neighbors would call for me to come get him, where I would find him backed into a corner, bug-shit out of his mind. He looked at me with murder in his heart, as if I was a stranger. Regardless of his small size, he tried his utmost to kill me. I came prepared with a thick leather jacket and long welder's gloves.

After a risky battle of doubtful outcome I stuffed him into a box, still growling and hissing. After a two minute ride home in the car, he settled down and when I tipped him out of the box in the front room, he shook his head, waggled his feet and strolled away as docile and unconcerned as ever. I would have to be a cat to understand that behavior.

In spite of his infirmities he still made it up onto the bed to sleep with us. We logged a lot of lap time over the years and every minute had to be paid for in grief when he died. We have been living at the bottom of the ocean this last week and are just now coming up for air.

Kathyrn does not handle grief very well. It is entirely within her character to get mournfully, grievously drunk and tumble headlong down the stairs, using up one of her nine lives. So far we have avoided that inconvenience.

I am ready for the hurt to end. Any time soon would be OK with me. The collective deep sighing around here draws such a vacuum indoors that it is hard on the weather stripping.

Rest well Harley, you knothead, you excellent friend. We'll see you again someday.

Neal

The Eulogy was written a week after the old boy left us. Since that time light and color have begun to come back into the world, food has taste again and we look out to the world and see that family, friends, and home mean everything to us.

Hawaii

Dear Friends,

Kathyrn and I have just returned from a vacation in Hawaii and I am pleased to tell you the islands are still out there waiting for you. But where they are, exactly, I don't know. I was reading the in-flight magazine on the way over, an article that insisted that the Islands were gliding along through the Pacific on a "tectonic plate" and scientists were quite sure that the whole archipelago had moved hundreds of miles, maybe more. Unsettling. I mean, here we are flying over a boundless and desolate ocean, hunting desperately for some islands that are known for not staying put! I can tell you I was greatly relieved when the pilot eventually found Oahu and guided us in for a landing.

Bless Kathyrn's pointed little heart; she got on the internet before our trip and found one good deal after another (one of us has to be organized). Kathyrn is the kind of person who has planned where she will be on the third Thursday of 2006, and I don't know where I will be tomorrow morning. She found a place to stay in pricey Honolulu for 35 bucks a night, the Plumeria Apartments. I admit it was a little scruffy: padlocks on the bedroom doors, and some guests who were probably fugitives from justice or out-patients at the tuberculosis clinic, but the low price freed up some money for other adventures. The resident manager may have been the poster model for "No shirt, No shoes, No service".

We didn't rent a car on Oahu, but got around pretty well on the bus system. Two dollars gets you out of tourist Waikiki, through industrial Honolulu (which doesn't exist if you read only travel brochures) and out into the farmlands and rural villages. Just a two hour bus ride acquainted me with the thoroughly laid-back side of rural life in Hawaii. To fit in as a resident, you need only a small bungalow, some chickens and a garden. Three or four rusted-out cars are a popular but optional accessory. I have several friends who hang loose in life (and you know who you are, Pete and Devan), who would be immediately assimilated into rural Hawaiian culture. A day after they stepped off the plane they would be wearing only shorts and flip-flops. They would have friends named Falolo and Moki, and they would know the secret handshake. I, on the other hand, after a month, would still be walking around with my Hawaiian shirt tucked in and wearing a Tropical Tourist Dork Hat, likely with the price tag still dangling from it.

My bus trip took me out to the north shore of Oahu where I had booked a glider ride at a quiet little airport below a range of bluffs. The pilot was friendly, but old, late seventies, maybe eighty, I'd say. "Probably better than some young pup just out of flying school," I thought.

He said "If we get some decent lift I could let you fly the glider some. We'll take the one with dual control." He buckled me in and signaled for the tow plane to take off. At 2000 feet we released the tow line and soared and banked as I snapped pictures of the surf line and green clad bluffs. A few minutes later, when the pilot was in the middle of explaining the operation of the stick and rudder to me I heard a shrill beep...beep...beep. He broke off with an abrupt "Oh No!"

"What's wrong?," I asked

"My pacemaker. The battery's run down." His speech had begun to slur and the glider yawed unsteadily. "You'll have to take her in... by yourself, kid. Good.... luck". With that, his head drooped forward and he lost consciousness.

76

Well! Wasn't this a pickle! But I kept cool. I made a few tentative movements of the controls to get the feel of flying the plane. I had read somewhere that the fastest way to burn off altitude and airspeed was to execute a loop so I put the glider into a steep dive until the airspeed reached redline, then pulled firmly back on the stick. Up, up, up, and over now, inverted at the top of the loop--- Gosh, these hills are even more beautiful seen upside down. Look at the color on that bougainvillea!---Into a dive now. Line up with the runway for landing. Easy now! Flare out for a perfect one-point landing (these gliders have but one wheel so all landings are done that way. I don't mean to brag).

As we rolled to a stop I opened the canopy and informed the ground crew of the emergency. They quickly popped a new battery in the pilot's pacemaker and in no time the old boy started to come around. I accepted the thanks of the ground crew and pilot, but turned down their offer of a luau they were willing to throw for me that evening. I had a bus to catch back to Honolulu. Hawaii was proving a very interesting place to visit! What will Kauai bring?

[The author's spouse wishes to interject something here: "My husband admits that parts of the foregoing may not stand up to the strictest standards of veracity. I don't know; I wasn't there, but I made him promise to give advance warning if his stories get this 'thrilling' in the future." K.F.]

We rented a car on Kauai because the bus system is minimal. After picking up the car, we drove off to explore the island, singing this song.

Down by the airport, early in the morning

See the little rental cars all in a row

Ours is a white one. All of them are white ones.

Credit card, beep, beep. Off we go.

I got so I could spot rental cars easily. They were all new, clean, and had no surfboard racks. Natives prefer big-tire Toyota pickups coated in red dirt and blistered with rust.

One of the pleasures of the trip was to put some slack key guitar music in the CD player and meander through hills planted with coffee, bananas, coconuts, and all those other exotic fruits Hilo Hattie said she would "squeeze all togeddah" when she was pitching Bali Hai wine on TV years ago

I was happy to see that the tourist centers were often contained in a small area and that you could avoid them or immerse yourself in them according to your preference. We went in for a mango and passion fruit Shave Ice at a weathered wooden store in a dusty village, then ten miles down the road we stopped at a time-share condo-ville big enough to have its own golf course and mall. It was there that I walked into an up-market gift shop and picked up a koa wood ukulele, boggled at the $1200 price tag, and set it down very, very carefully and scrammed.

Some beaches were deserted for miles, others had umbrellas and drink service from the hotel bar and at least one other beach was a semi-permanent tent community of young backpackers. The latter was a county park that had a scheduled "roust" on Tuesdays. All campers had to clear out to allow park maintenance. Most tents were back in the same places the next day.

One of my favorite authors, Bill Bryson, complained that in all his travels he had not found the quintessential tropical hotel: veranda's, potted palms, lazy ceiling fans, women in floral print cotton dresses and, sitting in the corner, Sidney Greenstreet and

Peter Lorre looking hot and shifty. I should send Mr. Bryson a card telling him that the Wild Ginger Inn in Hilo is the place he seeks. Messrs. Greenstreet and Lorre were away on some nefarious business, but all the other elements were there with the addition of a comfortable hammock, a pampered peahen strutting the lanai, and bananas to be picked off the stalk. The tropical downpour on the tin roof was enchanting in the afternoon, but damnable at 3:00 am.

The Merrie Monarch Hula festival in Hilo was high on our list of Sights To See and it proved to be all we wanted for music, dance, and local color. The TV stations gave it 16 hours of coverage and the stadium hall was sold out months in advance. At the opening ceremony a barefooted priest came out in red vestments and lei and offered a prayer in Hawaiian. Next, a woman sang the The Star Spangled Banner (in English) followed by a song in Hawaiian that I must assume was the anthem for the nation of Hawaii. A great many in the audience knew the words and sang along. I got the feeling that this was more than just the state song, that they regarded themselves as a separate people and not just America's 50th state. Across the street from the performance stadium stood half a dozen booths promoting a "give Hawaii back to the Hawaiians" message. Hawaii had once been an independent nation with a native monarch, and popular reverence for the last reigning king and queen was evidenced by the large portraits of them flanking the performance stage.

I was surprised by the number of people who spoke English as a second language. I struggled to understand the Asian and Pacific Island accents and pidgin English that were common, if not prevalent, everywhere I went. When I approached strangers to ask directions, shy Japanese girls covered their mouths and giggled, Chinese people imposed their rising and falling tonal patterns on English, and Hawaiian bus drivers were often terse, preferring hand gestures (friendly ones).

I was also surprised to see so many women in colorful muumuus. I had assumed that was just another travel brochure fiction, like lederhosen in our local Bavarian theme town. But no, they were as commonplace as Stetson hats and cowboy boots in Texas. Television has done so much to homogenize American culture, I lose sight of the fact that many regional clothing styles still persist. It's just that my own regional costume is based on muted colors, denim, and Gore-tex.

Like most tourists I had a hard time remembering Hawaiian place names. I gave up on trying to read street names as we whizzed by. They were all a blur of k's, l's, w's, m's and double vowels. However, the similarity that makes place names so perplexing is just the thing that makes it easy to sing in Hawaiian. Take a handful of syllables and link them together any old way and you have it. Try this:

Waki haole hoki poki

Pau kona koka kola

Pupu liki tiki mai tai!

I'll bet it means something perfectly beautiful. Put it to any tune you like, maybe "Tiny Bubbles" or "99 bottles of beer on the wall".

Kathyrn's travel trip: On a day of busy museum hopping, schedule a visit to a planetarium. The seats recline and it's cool, dark and relatively quiet.

"And rising in the east are the twin stars, Castor and.... What is that? That sound! Are you snoring? "Sorry, Dear"

Steep cliffs on Kauai's north shore prevent you from driving completely around the Island. Hanalei bay lies at the end of the road and the town definitely has that end-of-the-road feeling. We went there to visit a friend's brother who had just opened a restaurant in Hanalei. We introduced ourselves to Roger Kennedy and were treated to the best grilled fish taco west of the Pecos (or anywhere). Roger came to Hanalei in 1978, a young man with not much more than surfing on his mind. He is one of those people lucky enough to find his destiny and realize it. He bought a lunch wagon, parked it near a surfer's hangout, and started selling tacos to the beach crowd. When the best waves came in he shut down the grill and went surfing. His wife, Barbara, is the docent at the restored Waioli mission/museum on park-like grounds. Their thoroughly Hawaiian bungalow nearby is a priceless perquisite of her job.

Before our trip, my mother sent me a letter in which she advised me to "try the poi. It's delicious". She is not known as a practical joker, but she sneaked that one in on me. I agree with the general opinion that it is really purple library paste. I will recommend it to my Scandinavian friends as a side dish for their lutefisk. Other items I passed up were Spam, stacked in a six foot pyramid in one supermarket, and ten-packs of frozen turkey tails. I have always taken Spam as a bit of a joke, the Rodney Dangerfield of brand name foods. So when I spoke to a fellow bus passenger, I commented on his tee shirt with the SPAM logo in large yellow letters.

"Now, that says "Hawaii" to me", I said.

"I don't know why you would say that ", he answered, "Spam is good any where".

I'm only saying that he was serious about canned pork parts.

Get wet when you go to Hawaii; plan on doing something in the ocean. I know we are accustomed to a 15 minute life expectancy in the ocean here in the Washington, but think of it as a tropical aquarium you can pee in. I'll spare you lengthy descriptions of the schools of colorful reef fish I saw when snorkeling (there were plenty, some wearing calico patterns that must be one of God's little pranks). I was cautioned not to touch the sea turtles, but when one as big as wash basin swam by a foot away from my mask, I couldn't resist. I regretted it then, expecting it to sneak up behind me with a grab-ass game plan of its own. I also spotted the not-so-rare white-bellied walrus in swim trunks and the bikiniwahini, a delightful marine creature.

Mark Twain visited Hawaii in 1866 and wrote dispatches for the California newspapers. Collected into a book, they became Letters from the Sandwich Islands which I took with me and read as I visited the sites he wrote about. His description of the Kilauea volcano at night is worth repeating. Of a viewpoint on the crater rim Twain wrote:

"I turned to see the effect on the company and found the reddest-faced set of men I ever saw. In the strong light every countenance glowed like red-hot iron...The place below looked like the infernal regions and these men like half-cooled devils just come up on a furlough...The smell of sulphur is strong, but not unpleasant to a sinner."

The volcano has erupted and subsided many times since Twain's visit, and was quietly venting steam from a dozen fumaroles when we were there. The action, according to the park rangers, was down on the coast where lava was flowing into the sea. To see it we drove down a road called The Chain of Craters. We stopped at the first viewpoint to see a lesser crater, noting its size, depth, and lava forms. The next crater we came to got a shorter inspection, and the last three got barely a glance as I shot by, calling out "Now passing another hole in the dirt!". I could tell we had arrived at a Sight To See by the cluster of tour buses and rental cars, but still, I wanted a first-hand opinion. I stopped a family with two young kids and asked "How far is it to the lava fall?"

"Oh, round trip, I guess we walked two and a half hours", Dad replied.

"See anything when you got there?," I persisted.

"Just steam. The rangers won't let you up close enough to see flowing lava. We got some pictures though"

"Of steam?" I asked

"Yeah", Dad said, looking away from his family.

So we drove back up the Chain of Craters Road faster than we came down.

At the end of our vacation I was ready to come home. I staggered into the airport, suitcases bulging with the requisite souvenirs (ukulele and pineapples) and found a seat in the boarding area. I was surrounded by 40 high school students also waiting to board. There may have been only 20 of them, but they were frisky enough for double that number. Upon boarding, I took my accustomed seat in the squalling baby section (It seems to follow me around, so don't sit near me if you have the option). (Neal's travel tip: bring ear plugs.) The high school group entered the plane and at once the adult chaperones plopped into their assigned seats and settled in. The students, however, needed the next 40 minutes to solve the puzzle of who will sit next to whom.

"I'll sit next to Kasi and Lindsay but not if Damon is with

them", and so on.

It was more complicated than 3-D chess and the adults knew enough to keep out of it.

Before closing, I offer one last observation. While driving around the Big Island we passed a High School sign that read: Home of the Beavers. Beavers? Why had they chosen such a mascot when they had so many tropical choices? Take the sea turtle as an example. The cheerleaders certainly could have done something with that:

Go Turtles go.

Fight turtles fight.

Stomp 'em, romp 'em.

Bite, bite, bite.

Of course it is possible to go too far with the local mascot thing. Hawaii's favorite little reef fish wouldn't do at all. I'm talking about the Humuhumunukunukuapua'a;

"Gimme an "H

Gimme a "U"…

That's all the Hawaii report for now. Aloha.

Neal   copyright 2003

84

Marie goes hiking

Dear Friends,

Today I have a hiking story for you, told to me by my friend
Jerry. He had a house guest for the summer, Marie, a woman in
her 50's, only recently arrived in the Pacific Northwest from Ne-
braska. On her birthday, she decided to go for a day hike in the
Enchantment Peaks area in the Cascades, partly because of Jerry's
loving descriptions of the area, and partly because of the magic
in the name, "The Enchantments".

Marie drove east into the Cascades, following Jerry's directions. She got started late and it was already after noon when she
parked among the other cars at the trailhead. " Distances seem a
lot longer when you are going uphill", she later said, "especially
when you are walking." She made it to a viewpoint of encompassing beauty just in time to witness that extraordinary flat light
of late afternoon sun.

Afternoon sun, Hell, it was sunset! Where did the time go?
Marie jumped up and skittered down the trail, self-reproach in
every step. She was halfway down the trail when the blue light of
dusk gave way to dark night. Marie crawled along on her hands
and knees for a time, groping in the dark for the path, but, feeling
a steep precipice, she admitted that she was stopped for the night.
She backed up under an overhang of rock and trees, and settled
in to wait out the night .

It rained.

The rain turned to snow and sleet. She had only a sweater;
one that felt a little thin just then.

Cold and lost in the dark, Marie felt that prayer would do some good, so she prayed aloud. Perhaps silent prayer would have been better, because a cougar approached to see what was going on. She heard a growl and the stealthy step coming closer until it was but a few feet away. Marie began shouting the Lord's Prayer in her high, small voice and continued until the cougar went on its way.

After nine or ten fleeting hours, it was light enough for her to continue down the trail. The wrong way, it turned out. She made it nearly to the top again before she realized her mistake and turned around. She arrived at the trailhead parking area cold enough to be blue in places and thoroughly exhausted.

Marie's car keys were hanging in the ignition, locked in the car.

No one was around to witness, but Marie may have said a bad word. The solution was clear, even to Marie's dulled state of mind. She would have to break one of the windows out of the car to get home. She picked up a hefty rock, lifted it high over her head, and brought it down on one of the side windows.

Did I mention that Marie weighs about 85 pounds, and that she had as much strength left as an ailing canary? The rock bounced off of the glass on the first, second, and third tries. In a desperate mood, she sat down and prayed for help. She is quite good at praying, and often gets results.

Her prayers caused two young rock climbers to drive up just then and stop at the trailhead. They looked once at Marie and said, "Lady, you're hypothermic". They stripped off her wet clothes, stuffed her in a mummy bag and put her in their car with the heater turned all the way up. She felt sooooo good, but before she drifted off for a nap, she told them about the locked up keys and her efforts to break the window.

One of the climbers had an expensive new ice ax , and it was itching for trouble. He swung it down on Marie's door window so hard it should have gone right through, handle and all. Instead it glanced sideways and pranged a neat hole in the chrome trim and put an awfully expensive kink in the door post. The second swing was true and the window burst into 8000 little particles.

"We broke out the rear door window", he reported to Marie, "but we didn't find the keys."

"No keys?", said Marie, "What rear door? My car is a two door."

They had broken into the wrong car.

Of course, Marie's light colored two door Toyota sat, windows intact, not twenty feet from some poor bastard's light colored four-door Toyota, scatter-coated with glass.

By this time the climber had the hang of breaking and entering. Marie's window glass exploded into perfect bits, the keys were retrieved and Marie was free to go home. But she is a moral and ethical woman, so she wrote a note to the owners of the damaged car attempting to explain the broken window and leaving her name and phone number and that of her insurance company.

She hadn't been home very long when the phone rang. It was the owner of the damaged car.

At a later re-telling of her story, Marie said, "They weren't very understanding. In fact, they were quite irate"

That's Marie's story . There's not much more to tell, except that the insurance company had a hard time putting the case into the proper pigeon-hole. It wasn't truly an accident, nor was it an act of vandalism, and what, exactly, were the names of those two young men who broke the window, anyway. But Marie didn't tell their names. After all, they were only trying to help.

This story is true and as straight-up as I could tell it.

Your pal,

Neal

Hong Kong 1986

Let us now join Professor Peabody and Sherman in the Wayback Machine as we travel back to 1986 when Neal and Kathyrn visited Hong Kong.

Hong Kong 1986

I am sitting uneasily in my seat aboard a Jumbo Jet as it shrieks downward, aimed, I swear to God, right at a group of large buildings and the base of a mountain that is Kai Tak airport, Hong Kong. In a few seconds we are snaking between office towers, our wingtips close enough to kiss the walls on either side. Looking outside, I see into the office windows. A secretary sits hunched over her keyboard. A junior executive slurps tea as I whistle by at 200 mph. The usual crosswind must be in force today because we are making such a crabwise approach. We make a one-wheel touchdown, followed by the roar of determined engine braking and...if I live through this I promise that someday I will write about, telling it like it is.

How in the world did I get into this and why am I here? It is all Yun's doing.

My college friend, Yun Yip Chin sits on the top of a huge pile of money and success. He started TPC Courier service in the early seventies. He and a friend began by wrangling a contract to hand-carry bank documents back and forth between Hong Kong and LA. Now his business ranks just behind UPS and Federal Express.

Yun invited Kathyrn and me to come visit him in Hong Kong, airfare and lodging provided by his company. TPC owns a seat on a flight each way across the Pacific every day, and a courier occupies that seat, sometimes a paid employee, sometimes a traveler who is happy to get a free seat. All we had to do was show up at the airport, sign for a manifest of bagged cargo and release it to his agent in Hong Kong. Rats! I was hoping for a diplomatic pouch handcuffed to my wrist. Kathyrn flew one day. I flew the next.

Even in business class it is a crippling, twenty hour flight. Crunch Class looked unbearable. There is a stop in Narita, Japan long enough to straighten your bones out, then on to Hong Kong.

Hong Kong translates from Chinese as Fragrant Harbor, now a well-worn joke. Descending into Kai Tak airport, the aircraft ventilation system inhales the peculiarly tainted smog of the city and you get the punch line.

Yun loaned us the use of a studio apartment he keeps in the city. One of his early partners liked to entertain his girlfriends away from home and the apartment comes in handy for the occasional guest couriers like us. It was worn and 12 floors up, but any space in HK is good.

The influence of British Colonialism still showed in Hong Kong (Honkers to the Brit ex-pats). Bits and pieces of colonial architecture remain, Double decker buses run the downtown routes and a noodle shop advertised "English Breakfast" The English Breakfast turned out to be baloney and an egg, both fried, and lukewarm tea in an unwashed cup, which made me "Lay Down to Die" ill for the next four days. The double-decker buses were packed tight with uniformed Chinese schoolchildren, looking astonishingly uniform to my western perception; hair, clothes, book bags, all chosen to blend in rather than stand out.

I stopped in to a little corner deli, The Hong Kong equivalent of a 7-11, and bought a mylar wrapped snack. It might have been a hot dog; it might have been a Hum Bao. I never found out. This was back before I had much experience with microwave ovens. I put it into the microwave and set the timer. The microwave didn't like the mylar at all. It made zapping and popping noises as little lightning bolts ran all over the package. The proprietor rushed from behind the counter, shouting at me in Chinese. "Ging Ha chou kan wong! Gwei Lin ha Yao!" and shut the microwave off. Some teenagers girls snickered behind hands held to their mouths. I particularly resented his reference to me as a "White Devil".

Years before this trip, in Mazatlan, as I sat In front of my seaside hotel, a flatbed truck loaded with baskets of dinner rolls pulled up to a service entrance. Two young men leaped off the truck with a basket of rolls to deliver to the hotel restaurant, but one man stumbled, sending two hundred rolls bouncing and roll-ing across the pavement. The men hurriedly gathered them up and delivered them to the service entrance. At dinner that eve-ning, I inspected our rolls for gravel but left the rolls on the plate. Now, in Hong Kong, I had a similar feeling when a butcher's deliveryman tied two dozen pork tenderloins, unwrapped, onto his bicycle rack and pedaled off through the city streets mindless of mud puddle splatter and the rank blue exhaust of diesel buses, heading, no doubt, to the restaurant I was going to that night.

I loved the airy simplicity of the bamboo scaffolding that embraced the office towers under construction. These are office towers equal to those found in any American city. When the core of the building is nearly complete, the scaffolding is erected. A truck pulls up to the sidewalk and teams of Haka Chinese work-ers, many women, in their distinctive polished cotton pantsuits and conical hats worked alongside the men erecting bamboo scaffolding on the new glass faced office towers. I'm told it's an ethnic trade union. The woman on the sidewalk takes a 20' bamboo pole off the truck and hands it up to the worker above her. The pole is handed from one to another up 30 stories where it will be lashed into the growing framework. The work of lashing the poles together is serious business, performed by a strictly controlled union or guild. When complete it resembles the world's largest bird cage with a steel and glass bank tower inside. It hardly seems safe. Americans would demand inspected steel scaffolding with safety rails and net

Safety and strict cleanliness are American obsessions. I felt the lack of protective regulation when I walked past a man in Button Alley who was tempering jackhammer tips in the middle of the sidewalk: propane torch throwing a two foot jet of blue flame, hammer and anvil throwing sparks, and an unperturbed flow of pedestrian traffic around him with only enough space to keep from scorching your pants as you jostled by.

Every apartment building was festooned with clothes airing on bamboo poles projecting from each window. My theory is that they not drying after a wash, but are only airing out, contributing to the Fragrant Harbor smell I sensed on arrival. You may take it as the HK national flag. (The construction crane is the national bird). Oriental underwear, fish drying everywhere, even on the sidewalk, blended with the blue exhaust of Diesel buses give HK a tangible atmosphere.

I was invited to spend an afternoon with Yun. I met him at his office. We walked to where his Rolls Corniche was kept at the top of a multistory car park. Our routine for the next four stops was to drive down to street level on a dizzying spiral ramp, creep through three blocks of choked downtown surface street traffic, then spiral up the next car park. I tagged along while he shopped for a watch band (Rolex of course), CDs at an audiophile's store, a jade chop (a kind of signet seal) at an antique dealer, ending at a haberdashery, shopping for dress shirts. The clerks knew him and spread out a dozen styles to choose from. Yun ordered two dozen. "Cheaper than doing laundry on a long business trip", he told me. With shopping checked off, we made for the New world health spa where Yun has a membership. His plan was to turn me over to a series of spa employees for the full treatment while he disappeared to tend to other business. First came a vigorous wash at the hands of a chap built like a heavyweight wrestler. As I lay down on his table, he bucketed me over with soapy water. Using a stiff towel wrapped around his forearm he scrubbed me raw, occasionally holding his towel up to my face to show me how much of my skin he had removed. He took much delight in this, as if he was proud of his result or to say, "You so dirty, white man." Sufficiently clean now, I was sent off to the sauna to be parboiled in steam. After all I could take of the heat, I left for the pools, three of them, One was icy cold, another was just short of a rolling boil and the third was just right, thank you very much, Goldilocks. The just right pool was popular with several chubby Chinese millionaires betting on horse racing at Happy Valley Down via a large TV screen. I fancied Brown Beauty to show in the fourth, but the language got in my way and being barenaked, I did not have my wallet with me.

I briefly reunited with Yun on my way to the massage room. I was re-wrapped in my white terry robe. when a young woman in a brief gym suit asked me, "You Rike walk on back"? I looked to Yun for guidance. He said, "Say yes to everything" So, I like walk on back. She swung up onto the table top and using the grab bars on the ceiling to maintain her balance she trod up and down my spine for a good bone crunching. I must have needed more crunching than Yun, because he finished early.

What was left of me was wrapped up again, this time with a terry turban and led into a salon that seated 30 other likewise robed and turbaned men. I paced down the rows looking for my sponsor, feeling a little panicked that all the oriental faces began to look alike. In fact I missed Yun and found him on a second pass. I was offered a piece of chilled star fruit and a dram of cognac, followed by an ear swab.

Feeling a bit limp but refreshed, we set off for the city via a tunnel under the harbor. Hair slicked back, a little cognac buzz, air conditioning on, and cool jazz on the CD player, we got stuck in traffic three feet behind a diesel truck loaded with live pigs. Pigs who had just experienced their first reckless high speed truck ride down the New Territories road. Queasy pigs with nervous stomachs. Yun closed the fresh air vent, but the lesson came home. Wealth can buy a very good life but it can't completely insulate you from the rest of the world.

Money can buy you a place higher up the hill. I believe that the actual altitude of your residence governs the price, so that if you live atop an apartment tower that looks down, ever so slightly, on flats across the street, you are in a superior position. People there may have great wealth but little to spend it on: no sprawling estate, no horses. Fast cars are a joke in Hong Kong's traffic. Yun once had a Maserati but couldn't get it out of first gear in town. He had to drive it over to the New Territories to blow the carbon out, so he sold it.

We got away from the city for a day trip by train and ferry to tiny, poor, and arid Lan Chai Island, walking through the village past men in shirtsleeves and short pants playing Mahjong nois-ily in front of a tea shop. At the highest point on the island we lingered over the view of the vast, blue China Sea with mainland China on the horizon A tennis court stood at the top of the hill. Boys in white shorts and shirts playing tennis on a sunny day lent a civil touch. We descended past miniaturized cows on the hillside to the Beach of Lost Soles (10,000 flip flops had washed up from a lost cargo container). Out in the South China Sea, a gunboat patrolled. Poinsettia TREES and gourds fill in backyard gardens.

Back in the city, Kathyrn took the Star Ferry to Kowloon to bargain for jade. I was sick so I stayed at home. Yun gave me Hell for letting Kathryn go on such a dangerous buying trip on her own. Who knew? I was too far gone to know where she was adventuring off to.

When I had recovered, we had dinner on Yun at a Mongolian Hot Pot restaurant. This dinner was with wife/kids/nanny and is where Yun fed me the best of the pot with crunchy squid and prawns he had selected out of a big tank on the wall. Yun's wife drank some of the broth at end after the veggies had steeped. That Yun's father was there and was introduced to us was a great honor. Yun's Nanny is a Philippina like so many others. Yun says not to worry about dining manners; Chinese have none. True, there was a ring of grease on the carpet around the table from discarded bones. The Noodle Man takes center stage with a baseball bat-sized dough, folded and stretched until he has a thousand noodles. He bows and leaves. Yun remembered that Kathyrn liked Johnny Walker Black Label, and it was true, a younger rowdier Kathyrn did like it. A sideboy appears with a split of JWB and refills her glass after every sip.

I visited "Philippina square" on Sunday where nannies meet to commiserate about home and families. Yun gave his nanny a vacation back home every two years

Kathyrn dines on American packaged Swiss cheese and white bread sandwiches to avoid the sickies, except when out with Yun and family.

Take a trip up the STEEP cog tram to the top of Victoria peak that overlooks Hong Kong. Up in the cool, clear air you will find flowering trees that we get only as small shrubs in the U.S.

In some restaurants I saw plastic models of food on offer. In a cabinet in the foyer I found delicious looking plates of food made of plastic. You could inspect the plate, point, and order without having to look at a menu. That's an idea I would like to see used in this country.

I hoped that some chance meeting would put me face to face with Frank Pong, an industrialist I knew only by telephone conversations through business in Seattle. Mr. Pong would call me at work, and in perfect measured English tell me of his needs for another of his yachts he was outfitting. He had one for blue water ocean racing, one for local round-the buoys racing and one for pleasure cruising in the Philippines and the China Sea. I could imagine him tilted back in a great leather chair in an executive suite atop a towering office building. He owned steel mills in China. He would ask for me by name and spend as much time as he liked on an overseas call seeking advice about his yacht's electrical system. I learned that two of his sailboats were berthed at the Royal Hong Kong Yacht Club, so I popped round to have a look. I was met at the portico by a bejeweled and turbaned Sikh with a mustache waxed to sharp points. Dressed in the full Imperial kit, he was there to greet the Tai Pans and glare the riffraff into submission. . If you need a classy bouncer to keep the hoi polloi away you couldn't do better than a huge Sikh, one with a spiky, menacing mustache. The one at the Royal HK Yacht club looks like he could kick your nebbish ass down the stairs without ruffling his turban. Feeling somewhat riffraffish myself, I steered for more plebeian areas.

A small salute cannon sits near the flagpole. Of the Royal Hong Kong Yacht Club, Noel Coward wrote, "In Hong Kong they strike a gong and fire off a noonday gun, but only mad dogs and Englishmen go out in the midday sun. I had the satisfaction of hearing the gun fired before tottering off under the noonday sun.

I Tried Not To Go To Disneyland

Flying in over Orlando Airport I could see vast tracts of houses, blandly alike, the kind that give me the willies, houses packed tightly as building codes will allow. Interspersed through-out the landscape were hundreds of ponds and lakes. Tract homes, wetlands, and forests of short pines were the signature landscape of Florida and nowhere a mountain, hill, or even a hump of high ground

Kathyrn and I had come to visit our lifelong friend Deidra, but she was working swing shift for The Mouse (Disney) that night and was unable to pick us up at the airport. Instead she sent a chauffeur and white stretch limousine. Deidra just natural-ly does things with great style. Chilled champagne anyone? We popped the cork on a bottle of "Faerie Castle", Disney's private label, before we left the parking lot. The limo was a Prom Date Special, down to the blue neon woo-woo strip lighting set into the onyx Corian bar top. We glided along the freeway pretty well oblivious to everything but the champagne and the sun setting like a red rubber ball.

Deidra lives in one of the tract homes I saw on the flight in. I felt the same unease I always feel in those places, maybe because I got lost in a tract home development a few years ago. On that occasion I hadn't paid much attention on the way in and the next night I had to find the house by myself late at night. I easily found the entrance to Graystone Pointe or whatever the hell the development was called, but then I got in trouble. I drove slowly down Brittney lane, Chelsea drive, Jason Court, and several other avenues named for the developer's grandchildren, but the curving lanes wound on and on with each house and yard exactly alike, all muted shades of gray, with approved shrubbery and mailboxes exactly alike. Even the cars were nondescript. Not so much as a plastic flamingo or distinctive birdhouse made any house stand out from its neighbors. After 40 minutes of driving around I was greatly relieved to recognize a doormat that was unique to my hosts' home.

I must keep in mind that Deidra doesn't mind living in a house that looks like her neighbor's She loves her little house, and it shows inside. She would probably feel isolated on acres of rural land. A strong advantage is price; she paid $84,000 for an 1100 square foot 2 bedroom, 2 bath home. In Washington that will get you a tiny "fixer-upper" in Rat City. In San Francisco that would be a modest down payment.

Almost every house in Deidra's development had a "bird cage" screened patio, many large enough to enclose a small swimming pool, but even these showed few signs of human occupation. Where were the potted plants, kid's toys, and barbecues, anything to show me this wasn't a movie set? I did see a garden hose coiled and hanging on a rack outside one house, but that was about the extent of the real-life clutter I saw.

During my visit, my usual routine was for me to drop Deidra off at her work where she books vacations on Disney's cruise line. On the way to work one morning I asked about the badge and Disney shirt she wore. Her answer informed me about the Disney dress code at her office and included this list:

Hair must be a natural color. No purple, of course, but also no obvious highlights or streaks.

Each earlobe may be pierced once. No other body piercings allowed.

Clear fingernail coating only. No red polish or long nails.

Dark skirt or pants

Disney uniform shirt

Photo ID badge

Makeup, nylon hose, shoes, shirts, etc. were also narrowly prescribed.

If you grew up wearing a Catholic school uniform you would be right at home.

Uniformity and regimentation were themes for me on this trip. The spookiest of these phenomena isn't even on the Disney World premises, but in a Disney-spawned community near the park called Celebration. It is a planned (over planned) community where wealthy and slightly demented people live. Celebration was all too tidy and perfect. No rowdy youths (actually no youths at all unless they had come to visit Nana and Gampa.) Restaurants and boutique shops abound and many of life's refined necessities are available, but you have to go beyond the town boundaries to get a new muffler put on your car, and a Wal-Mart would be unthinkable. Kathyrn refused to stop in Celebration for lunch and went back to the car to wait for me as I explored. As I was walking along the man-made canal I realized I was listening to music. It was emanating from speakers hidden under the bushes. At that point I choked on this eerie preserve of orderliness and happily went back to the world of strip mall hamburger joints.

There are 150 fast food joints along the perimeter of Disney World and while sitting in one of them I got to wondering how the imagination and creativity that marks Disney World could come from such a rule-bound pool of employees. The look-alike housing and dress code spoke of such uniformity that I wondered where Disney could recruit the extremely creative people for the Imagineers, the staff that invents the things that make Disney Corporation famous. They must be living in Key West, Maui, or Aspen. I would have liked such a creative job but I don't see myself in a Mickey Mouse shirt with an ID badge pinned to it. Oh well, no great loss probably; the Disney attractions I would have created would have been a little too strange for old Walt. I'm talking about attractions that aren't safe and sanitized, something that gives you a good story to tell when you get home: your wife's butt gets pinched in "Old Italy", a ride where you get to drive a taxi in Manhattan (only the cars aren't on tracks), a band of gypsies pick your pockets. You get the idea.

MANATEES

Kathyrn and I wanted to see some of natural Florida. Kathyrn wanted to see a manatee in the wild but they had migrated farther south for the winter. However, we thoroughly enjoyed seeing one in the Sarasota aquarium.

I can save you the trouble of going to Florida to see a manatee:

Borrow a friend's sleeping bag. A dark gray mummy bag is best.

Toss it in a swimming pool and let it soak and swell.

Scatter a bunch of lettuce leaves on the surface of the pool.

Get in the sleeping bag with just your face sticking out and nibble on the leaves

Voila! You look just like a real manatee.

Fart now and then; the kids will love it.

SANIBEL

We drove 4 hours to the Gulf Coast community of Sanibel Island, accessible by a causeway and bridge. Its attraction was a long undeveloped beach littered with shells. Shell collecting has been a lifelong hobby with Kathyrn and she spent several hours walking the beach while time was suspended and replaced with delight.

Sanibel Island is largely devoted to resort homes and rentals. Commerce seemed to consist of restaurants, gift shops and realtors. From the look of the homes and inhabitants I would bet that the waitresses that served us can't afford to live there, but commute from the working town of Fort Myers. I liked the bike paths which wound through the palms and bougainvillea, well away from the car traffic. I also understood why no one in Florida needs a bicycle with more than one speed. The state is as level as a pool table (and the climate can turn a 21-speed gear train into a heap of flake rust in a week)

Florida is so flat that whenever some builder needs a hump of dirt to build a foundation or a highway overpass, the earth must be excavated or "borrowed" from some other flat area, creating what are known as "borrow ponds".

ALLIGATOR

I wanted to see an alligator on this trip and I thought I would have to go see one at Goober's 'Gator-Rama and Air Boat Thrill Ride*, but a local wild alligator obliged by making an appearance. Only 200 feet from Deidra's house is a small pond with a resident alligator. A muddy slide showed where he had been in the habit of coming out of the pond. The alligator was about 6 feet long and weighed 60 pounds and was a little less lively than the manatee. A Sign at water's edge advised everyone to keep small pets on a leash.

*I made that name up but I was sorry to miss visiting a similar, but real, place named Lone Cabbage Fish Camp.

PROPERTY CONTROL

Deidra took us on a back lot tour of Disney World partly to spot wild armadillos. We sighted no armadillos but we did cruise past many large industrial buildings like those that usually produce boxcars or fiberglass septic tanks elsewhere in the real world. Here I caught glimpses of a Disney replica Viking ship, artificial rocks and trees and a row of man-sized Chip 'n Dale figures.

We went to Property Control, an unadvertised store on the back lot of Disney World. Their stock was mostly surplus clothing and knickknacks from the Disney souvenir stores, but also scratched and dented fixtures from the resorts and vehicles past their useful life. Lost and found items completely filled one corner of the store. One bin contained blue velvet graduation caps, the traditional mortar board, only with mouse ears. They were from Disney University where employees receive training before they are allowed to work in the park.

BORDERS TO THE KINGDOM

After Disneyland got going strong in California the corporation slyly began buying up land near Orlando at cheap prices using front companies and never mentioning the Disney name. In this way they acquired thousands of acres and were able to form their own little government, like Vatican City, only with a Mouse instead of a Pope. The result is that non-Disney tourist schlock sprawls for miles along the border of Disney property. You drive into the park leaving behind all the Krispy Kreme Donut joints and knock-off tee shirt shops, and pass though a mile of relatively natural looking woods and wetlands before you see any Disney park development. Disney was able to plan and build its complex from the beginning, infrastructure and all. The sewage produced at the park is sent to a processing plant where it is spread out and disked under several times in fields and allowed to sterilize before being used in landscaping as fertilizer. It is known as "Mickey Mud"

DISNEYSPEAK

Disney Corp. is very careful with their terminology. The correct translations are:

Vacation Club = timeshare condo

Attractions = Rides

On or Off Property = within the park boundaries

Cast members = employees. You are a cast member even if you are a cashier at a hot dog stand. Cast members like Snow White, who do not wear a mask, are called face characters,

Remember, it is Walt Disney World in Florida – not Disneyland.

CASTAWAY CAY

Deidra works at a large office complex housing 3000 other Disney employees. She books cruises on the Disney Cruise Line. Their southern terminus is Castaway Cay in the Caribbean, a low lying island which was formerly a stopover on the drug smuggling route, though that is not prominently mentioned in Disney's brochure.

A DAY AT THE PARK

During a week of visiting and local sightseeing I had avoided actually going into the park. But with a last day left unscheduled and a free pass in my hand, I went. I spent the day on trains boats and trams getting an overview of Disney World but keeping it at arm's distance.

EPCOT

I think Disneyland succeeded best in creating Fantasyland, Toon Town and other decidedly unreal venues, but I was disturbed by their recreations of places that exist in real life. The Many Lands exhibit at Epcot is an example. 15 different cultures are represented in this part of the par, each on 400 feet of lake front footpath. Here and there were a cutsie-wootsie Merrie Olde England, a severely sanitized Moroccan Souk, and a bit of India that was looking particularly polished up and well fed. While in Merrie Olde England I stopped for a lunch of fish and chips at the Rose and Crown. A hostess in Elizabethan peasant blouse and skirt greeted me while staying in contact with the Maitre' D' via the communications headset she wore under her mobcap. That jarred me as did the fake crack in the liberty bell in Liberty Square.

NASCAR

As I was leaving the park, I could hear, just on the other side of a line of trees, the one attraction I actually wanted to go on, Richard Petty's Nascar Experience: shockingly noisy, powerful race cars roaring around a banked oval track. It wasn't Disney and it wasn't fake. It was real and sounded dangerous. Unfortunately it also cost $300 bucks. I was tempted briefly, but instead decided to abuse the rental car on the drive home.

Yeeee Haw!

Hugs and Howdys to you all,

Neal

Last Chapter for Uncle Dig

My Uncle Dig was lost in WWII, and I mean really lost. His bomber was shot up over the northern Kurile Islands north of Japan. For 50 years none of us knew what had become of him. Had he crashed into the sea or been taken prisoner? We only knew what the government telegram said, "missing in action and presumed dead" I can now write the last chapter.

At uncle Dig's crash site in Kamchatka, the U.S. Central Identification Lab found and returned some bones and artifacts from the wreck of Bomber 31. Eventually news was released that three crewmen had been identified, my uncle among them. The fate of the other four is unknown, but the Navy offered funerals with military honors for all.

The Navy has a program of paying the travel expenses for a limited number of family members to attend a military funeral, and by this means I flew to Eureka, California, my home town, for Dig's interment. I was amazed to find that a Navy Mortuary Travel Affairs Office existed at all, and more amazed to find them located in Illinois. They shipped my airline tickets immediately, even offering to pay my meals and lodging. I thanked them but explained I had a binding agreement to stay at my mother's house and eat at her table, and to do otherwise would put me in dutch with her.

Veteran's Day in Eureka

Dig's service was held on a rare sunny day at our family's cemetery.

Two well-spoken sailors with shined shoes and crisp salutes presented the small urn they had escorted over from the identification lab in Hawaii and a chaplain read a military service and prayer. Our family had long held out hope that Dig had survived, as an internee or P.O.W., and in memory of that hope, a popular song of the war years, "Homecoming Waltz" was played, which proved to be a little more than most of the elders could handle dry-eyed. All the while, I could hear a salute squad of retired vets rehearsing their moves outside the chapel. "Fooorrd Harch! Hup, Hoo, Hee, Ho". At graveside they fired a well done 21 gun salute, well done especially for a squad of duffers my age who last fired a weapon in earnest during the Vietnam War. The visiting sailors gave a salute in exaggerated slow motion, folded a flag for presentation, and tucked three spent cartridges into it. A trumpeter standing at a distance played "Taps" to conclude the ceremony.

A similar ceremony was scheduled for Arlington National Cemetery a week later. Only a few family members were invited to fly on the Navy's purse, so if I was to go it would be without the Navy's support. Let me now thank my friends who encouraged and helped me go: my neighbors who came forward to offer some bonus air miles, a plan which was unfortunately thwarted by the short notice, a friend of my cousin who generously provided me with standby tickets, Devan Miller who drove me to Seattle, my brother Richard who let me share his motel room, though I am known to be a champion snorrer, and Kathyrn, who supported my going and drove to Bainbridge to pick me up at the ferry.

Arlington National Cemetery

A young Navy commander met our party at our motel and drove us to Arlington Cemetery. We, and families of the other six lost crewmen, were shown to reserved pews in the chapel.

The service was brief and by the book. A flag draped casket representing all of the crewmen stood near the altar during the ceremony and was carried by Navy pallbearers out to a waiting caisson. I don't think any of us anticipated the extent of the honors, but the staff at the chapel are smartly turned out and well prepared for funeral formality. The caisson was drawn by six black horses with riders all in full kit: head plumes for the horses and riding boots for the soldiers. A 40 piece military band stood at attention, then struck up an unexpectedly lively march, and led the procession of mourners from the chapel.

At graveside I stood some distance apart to get a picture of the gun salute squad with the Washington monument in the background. The traditional three salvos were fired with machine-like precision while my brother and cousins sat at graveside with 20 or 30 other mourners. I can't say what the others were thinking, but we all instinctively ducked down a few inches when four screaming F-116 Tomcats flew over in the "lost man formation". I had seen this before as a set piece in air shows, but I felt its real significance as the "lost man" pilot veered off on his own, parting from his squadron.

After the ceremony the families were directed to an auditorium where we had an opportunity to introduce ourselves, meet other families and share stories, a fine closing to the service.

Arlington Cemetery is too large to see in a single sweep, a marble farm of headstones dating back to the Civil War. Clarence "Dig" Fridley's marker is flanked by thousands of graves beyond count. On the other side it faces a broad, empty lawn that is filling up with new graves even now.

Sights and Side Trips in D.C.

I arrived in downtown Washington, D.C. late at night with

109

a hike of five blocks to the hostel where I had reserved a room. I repeated "It can't be the Homicide Capitol of the U.S." like a rosary as I walked, but in fact the streets were cleaner and less threatening in that neighborhood than many in Seattle. I checked in at the hostel and went to my room, a small space entirely filled with eight bunk beds, six of which contained sleeping Japanese young men. They would awake in the morning wondering if it was the white guy that snored all night or was it a dozen diesel buses revving their engines in the street below. I slept like a dead man, and that is all I asked for my $26 room rate.

I love the D.C. subway! It's clean, fast, cheap, and handy. Why can't Seattle have one? My only problem was the drivers who call out the stops as if their mouths were full of mashed potatoes. It sounded like this (with added tinny speaker static): "Woodle doodle farble numby and absolutely last chance to transfer to Mumbleton, Garbleville, and Whateverly."

It was a small revelation to me to watch TV news of the nation's capitol as a local event. Channel 3 would go live and remote covering a presidential motorcade and outside you might hear the motorcycle escort sirens on the freeway. I visited Arlington Cemetery on the 40th anniversary of JFK's assassination and learned later from Channel 5 that Kennedy family members had been there to leave flowers at his gravesite.

After bureaucracy and hotel keeping, the third major industry in D.C. is security. I hope to never again see so many security guards, sentinels and rent-a-cops. At Smithsonian Museum buildings you must pass through a metal detector and open your bags for search. At the Washington Monument the grounds were under construction for"beautification", according to the ranger. The project consisted largely of a high concrete wall and anti-tank barriers. At least the barriers in front of the Museum of Natural History were 1-ton concrete tubs planted with geraniums. There are eight windows at the top of the Washington Monument, but four of them were clumsily closed off with a plywood door and padlock. This was done to accommodate security cameras that surveyed the capitol mall, but it made the waiting lines for viewing twice as long.

Everyone finds some artifact at the Smithsonian Museums that speaks to them or touches their interest. For a motorhead like me it was the Spirit of St. Louis. It was the genuine article, and close enough at hand that I could almost reach out and touch it…If you held me while I leaned out over the balcony…Before the security guard came.

Beware of Museum Overload. It happened to me in the Gem and Mineral wing. After gawking at thirty display cases of awesome rarities I found myself passing by a 400 pound amethyst and an emerald the size of a coffee urn with barely a hurried glance.

The rotunda of the Natural History museum features a monstrous bull elephant, poised to charge, trunk raised in full toot and with a wild gleam in his glassy eye. But even at the end of the day, weary of wonders, I had to return for another long look at him. I named him Tootles.

I will close with this final item: As I was flirting with a pretty flight attendant on the trip home, I asked in a whining voice "Are we there yet? How many more miles? Her answer, in a stern Dad's voice: "If you ask me one more time I'm turning this plane around and you're going back to Baltimore." Bless her heart.

I was glad to go on this trip. I was ecstatic to return.

Neal

Marlin Fishing in Mexico

In 1972 I took a motorcycle trip down the newly completed Baja Peninsula road. I rode buddy with my father on his BMW and my brother rode solo on his Gold Wing. We saw way more desert than I ever want to see again, especially those cactus that stand with their arms pointing up like men marching in thousands to the horizon.

At La Paz, the southern tip of the peninsula, we took the ferry from to Mazatlan on the mainland. We recuperated for a day or two in a beach front hotel planning what to do next. One of the many vendors and touts working the tourist beaches sold us on a fishing trip for the company he represented. We were all astute and wary bargainers and asked what we were getting for our money. Under examination, he assured us that the boats were modern and safe, the captain was well qualified and experienced.

Just a few more questions I said. "Will a gourmet lunch be served?"

Si, Senor.

I want my father's to catch the biggest marlin of the day.

OK, Senor

And I want my brother to catch one bigger than that.

He nodded enthusiastically

And I want mine to be bigger than either of theirs.

Si, Si Senor.

113

Well, how could we refuse?

The three of us showed up at the marina the next morning and were assigned a boat.

The captain and the bait boy were Mexicans in their mid twenties, in well worn and faded jeans and tee shirts. Though they were cordial, there was also a feeling of being processed and let's get the day over. The boat was also well worn and faded, a fiberglass no frills 26 foot cabin cruiser. The captain carried a boat compass, which he kept wedged in a corner of the fly bridge with his foot.

I figured we would be lucky to catch any fish at all, but was quite contented to cruise around on a sunny day and drink beer. I am puzzled to this day about what happened about the beer. The captain warmed up the engine, the bait boy put the bait and lunch aboard, and we boarded and were off. As we were about to pass the breakwater the captain announced that he forgot to bring the beer. It was not a very well acted line. My guess is that he always "forgot" the beer. Whether it was the expense, because beer in Mexico is not particularly cheap, or whether his day goes smoother when the clients are sober I don't know, but the day looked to be a dry one.

We settled into a routine of motoring around a few miles offshore at cruise speed looking for a good spot to go fishing. The captain and bait boy knew what to look for and we had no clue so we just sat quietly. After an hour or so, the captain called out "Marlin!" and hit the throttle, heading for a spot a half mile away. What he had seen was a marlin's bill just above the surface resting at a shallow angle, looking like a stick.

It turned out that that day was not the best fishing day of the year, but possibly the worst. The water was unseasonably cold and murky and the moon had been full the last few nights, so the marlin had been feeding at night and were absolutely stuffed, too gorged to do anything but lay on the surface digesting. We were handed rods with feather lures while the captain positioned the boat to make a pass near the marlin. We trolled by it this way and that, once even dragging the line across its bill. No response. The marlin was in a coma from overeating. The bait boy reeled in our lines and rigged big treble hooks. We made a few more passes using our hooks like grapnels hoping to snag the fish in the body, but the fish settled slowly down out of sight. We had similar experienced twice more during the day and we were starting to show signs of boredom.

The captain, who had been watching us, judging when he could suggest going home, gave another call "Tortuga" and changed direction to show us what he found: a two foot long sea turtle. He asked us,"Senors, this turtle is illegal to catch, but if you don't care too much we would like to take it." OK with you?" It helps to feed our families."

In 1972 we were not very conservation minded, or maybe we were bored and wanted to see something new, so we gave our assent. The crewman quickly gaffed the turtle and brought it aboard, butchering it on the deck. He packed the meat in a bucket and cleaned the shell. He stowed the meat and shell out of sight back in the engine space. And we were off for home.

At least there were no other fishermen posing beside marlin hung up by the tail at the landing. The captain and crew live by tips I suppose, but a no-fish day is a small tip day, and on a day with no beer I was even less generous.

Maybe Ernest Hemingway could have made a good story out of a day like that

Mr. Fridley's Math Pop Quiz

Nancy is baking a batch of snickerdoodles. Liz has added 1/3 cup of flour to the batter already, but the recipe calls for 1-3/4 cups. How much more flour must Nancy add?

Whoa, Dude! Fractions are tricky! You go messing around with Common Denominators and you're gonna wind up with dumplings for sure.

Answer: Just keep adding flour until the dough isn't sticky, but not really dry either. Roll out and cut into circles.

Bake at 190° C for 10 minutes

Uh-oh, how much is that in Fahrenheit?

Hint: use the formula: 5/9 x °C + 32 = °F

Multiple Choice Answer:

A.   Go to Canada and buy a stove with a Celsius scale.

B.   Ask your Mom. She likes to help you with algebra problems

C.   375°F. You always bake cookies at 375.

D.   Snickerdoodle dough is great raw! Why mess with baking?

Neal's Rules for Writing

These aren't your rules; they're mine   You should make your own list. What I mean is that I have identified persistent flaws in my writing style which I need to keep hammering on.

1. Show, don't tell. "He was very tired." Is telling me he was tired. "He mumbled hello and flopped onto the sofa. His next sentence ended in a snore." Shows me he was tired.

2. Read it from your reader's point of view. Have you made assumptions others don't have?

3. Have you expanded the interesting parts fully? Don't hide your story with modesty. Don't leave out the juice. We hear "Don't be so dramatic. Don't toot your own horn." Kill that impulse. In writing you have the advantage of a longer audience attention span than you have in conversation. If you felt something strongly did you convey it?

4. Use all of your senses, not just visual. What did the scene smell and sound like? Use hearing and touch too.

5. Choose active voice over passive.

6. Review for continuity, flow, and transitions.

7. After expanding the piece to tell your story fully, cut every word that is not working hard. Highlight the very best parts. Consider leaving out all else.

8. Try recording the story as you tell it. Compare it with the written piece. You may find that the vocal version was stronger, more alive   Read the piece aloud. If you have written something

that is not in your character it will jump out.   Reading aloud also improves sonority and reveals awkwardness.

9. Write to a specific audience, not a "general public".   Imagine your friends gathered around as you write. Who will appreciate this or that part?

10.   Review for punctuation, grammar, and spelling. There's no glory in this chore. Get it right and no one notices. Get it rong and you look like an idoit.

11.   Kill the clichés. Do the hard creative work to make a new phrase, simile, or metaphor.

12.   Vary the pace and intensity. You can't gallop all the time nor can you always rest and savor the scene.

13.   Take out the "I"s. Change me, me, me. To "You"

14.   Turn off your "Editor" when doing the first draft.

New Year's Day 2002

I'm standing by my front window trying to decide if I should feel a little gloomy or positively cheery. The view from my window is of the stark rocks and snow of Hurricane Ridge, clamped between a sunless gray sky above and the dark green and shadow of the winter forest below. Tee shirt weather is a distant memory and the fish in the pond wait, still, beneath the ice.

Before I fall completely into an emotional hole here, let's turn around and view the happy scene in my living room. Harley Big Cat is curled up like a croissant, centered in the rush of warm air from the pellet stove. Kathyrn is sleeping in late, snoring like a dragsaw, and our chubby cat Samba is crouched on top of her. Norman Rockwell, come and paint this contented scene.

I watched a videotape of my 54th birthday from 10 months ago. It was a rippin' good party, held in the shell of our half-built house. The guests all brought something for "Show and Tell" and the video shows Sandy Smith teaching us the Macarena in a room with just bare studs, no insulation and the pellet stove blazing. It was a cold night in February and the temperature inside topped at 50 degrees. The video tape is a record of our friends having fun, but it also reminds me that, yes, really, we have made progress building and even though a whole week is sometimes spent doing a simple task, we now have four rooms finished and two to go.

So there you have it; building this house is my life and I could write the rest of this letter about my education as a house builder. My last two years have been spent learning house building by the trial and error method:

Make a trial

Screw up, Big Time

Clean up the mess

Read the instructions this time, dummy.

Make another trial after my back, knees, and attitude have recovered.

Call it good enough and move on.

Bumpy though that process has been, Kathyrn has seen more tumult this year. Her year began, as usual, working at the radio station for the blind in Seattle. She was home at The Dirt on weekends and living in a depressing little rented room in the big city, weekdays. Her friends at work are as caring and friendly a group as you will find anywhere, but the sum was that Kathyrn had no life in the city and just a refuge here at The Dirt.

She quit. Retired. Vamoosed. And for the next few months held the unenviable position as apprentice laborer to me, General Contractor. In her former situation she was surrounded by people who respected her knowledge and skill in a well organized municipal agency. The following week she was a hod carrier and broom pusher, camped on a construction site with only me for company. If you happened by that summer and found us up on ladders or down in a trench calling each other unpleasant names, that was our Period of Adjustment.

I am happy to report that Kathyrn has now hit her stride as an interior decorator and landscape architect. Now I am Hiram the Helper, whose job it is to dig and carry and stand by the wall, holding a heavy mirror while Kathyrn directs that it be moved up and down, left and right by infinitesimal increments. And I'll tell you, it has been a rocky Period of Adjustment.

We have been packratting housewares for years, Kathyrn specializing in decorative Foofoo, and it was shocking to find out how much stuff we had. We will have to build another house to store it all. As it is, this project has grown from a few attic rooms over a garage to "Martha Stewart, eat your gizzard". I obviously get a lot of fun from grumbling about what a trial this has been, but when I open the door and walk in to that sunny living room and look around , I always find something that pleases me deeply.

Our neighbors have been a blessing we didn't expect when we bought the property years ago: campfires in the summer, pressing cider in the fall, visits and parties around Christmas. They have all been eager to help one another and many times they have given their time to help me with building. They have learned to be wary, though. On a casual stop by for chitchat they know there is likely to be a refrigerator at the base of the stairs waiting for hands enough to move it up into the kitchen. Last summer I walked around the neighborhood loop, trolling for laborers, and found a full crew, ready to try their hand at plastering when the living room walls needed to be finished. I truly value the mark of many hands in the plaster from that day

We have taken a few breaks from building. Once, we went with good friends to the little Bavarian theme town of Leav-enworth in the Cascades during one of those curious breaks in the summer when the town was not surrounded by forest fires. Instead they were having an accordion festival, which many people agreed was preferable to a forest fire. The 40-member Ulster (Northern Ireland) Marching Accordion Band had bussed in from Toronto, Canada and were ready to party. They marched and played through town, performed a concert in the park, and afterward, gathered at King Ludwig's Rathskeller up the street, where the real entertainment started. I had inspected King Lud-wig's earlier in the day; their main claim to fame was barbecued Schweinhoxen (swine hocks, if that makes it sound more appealing). Put a dozen accordions up on a tiny stage, serve beer in liter steins and pack the place with Irishmen, and let the good times roll. I was surprised to see many German-Americans there. The whole Bavarian theme started out as a Chamber of Commerce promotion back in the 50's when the town was failing, but it caught on with Germans who were living in the Northwest, missing the Alps and Oom-pah culture. So they were all there, Irish and Germans, rocking back and forth in their seats, arms linked, and singing about the Golden Rhine and Galway Bay.

Kathyrn and I wanted to fly down to Eureka for a Christmas visit with the home folks, but I decided to drive instead. It wasn't the risk of airline terrorism that drove the decision, but air travel inhospitality. I am old enough to remember when airline travel was enjoyable, and have grown to dislike airport mentality as it has changed over the years. Rather than be frisked and treated as a suspect, I'll go by car when I can. Besides, there was the attraction of the drive along the Oregon coast in winter.

We drove 1500 miles with the windshield wipers on, gaped at breaking surf that stretched out toward Hawaii, and reckoned our prospects for fresh Dungeness crab that would be just coming in at Humboldt Bay.

In the middle of a week of storms, we detoured out to Cape Blanco to see if it was breezy. I can tell you that rain in 50 knots of wind has a deep-cleansing effect. Put your jacket on before you get out of the car.

In Eureka we found that the weather had kept all the crabbers in port. We were told that if we showed up at the dock around 5:00 PM, we could buy some right off the Becky Lou when she came in. Success! We had crab cakes, crab sandwiches and crab cocktails to satisfy. My mom was an eager participant in all this and is doing well, I'm happy to say. She can barely totter around with her walker, except when invited out to a restaurant. No need to ask twice, she has her purse and coat in hand.

I recommend having a steelhead fisherman in the family on these occasions. My nephew, Deputy Mike, is fully prepared and willing to perform the Magic Secret Steelhead Barbecue, even on a wet December evening. He has perfected bringing an entire dinner in a basket over to my Mom's house. He is presently assigned to the Sheriff's Marine Unit, proud possessors of a retired Coast Guard 44' motor lifeboat. He gave us a tour of Humboldt bay on the department's newly spiffed-up boat. Eureka is so much like Port Angeles; one pulp mill limping along, deserted log export docks, and a fishing fleet that hasn't been able to afford to paint their boats for years. People ask me why I bothered to move.[1]

Kathyrn said her back couldn't take long days on the drive home, so we shopped our way home over the next four days. If we passed a place that made cheese, we saw the cheese, when we passed a place that made burl knickknacks, we shopped for burl; the same for smoked salmon, , antiques, myrtlewood, petrified whatever, and more antiques. We eventually did get home and had ourselves a merry little Christmas right here at The Dirt, and that's why this is a late New Year's letter rather than a timely Christmas one.

That's the Dirt Report for now. I wish for you Health and Prosperity in the new year, and if either of those are in short supply, I wish you Happiness.

Yer Pal, Neal

---

1   Port Angeles actually has a summer

Neal's Recipe for BBQ Pork. (From Scratch)

For the first years I lived on Vashon I commuted off-island to work, but like many others wished I could find work close to home. That's why I accepted the job of day custodian at the island's middle school

I hadn't been on the job long before someone in the teachers room asked me how I felt about pigs. "I'm fine with pigs", I said wondering where the conversation was headed. It was explained to me that my predecessor in the job had raised a pig each year on cafeteria scraps, and roasted it at the end-of school teacher's party. Would I like to do the same? I gave it some thought and decided that it would be easy enough and a new experience, so, yes, I would do it. Where could I find a starter piglet?

In Seattle, you look next to the airport. The next time you fly in to Sea-Tac airport, in the last seconds of final approach, look down carefully at the tree and brush lined valley north of the landing strip. It's a secret livestock ranch, with many breeds of barnyard animals hidden here and there in little coops, pens and corrals. I took the ferry to Sea-Tac and began hunting for the "ranch"

After roaming, lost, among the bushes and lean-tos I came across a house so run down I mistook it for a barn. A brawny wrinkled woman came out to see what I wanted. She led me to an especially muddy pen which contained several large car hoods propped up on blocks. I had asked for two weaner pigs, and these were cowering in some numbers under the hoods. The woman stuffed her skirt hem into her boot tops, climbed over the fence, and made her attack. It didn't go smoothly. Crouching in the muck and halfway under the car hood, she reached and wrestled with half a dozen little pigs until she had a firm grip on one. This was not suffered in silence by the herd in general. She lifted up one muddy, very excited piglet and sacked it, and with even more ruckus, brought out my second squealer. She stuffed my cash payment in her shirt pocket, chose not to offer me a mucky handshake, and I was a pig owner.

I put each piglet in its own gunny sack in the trunk of my car and headed for the ferry. Squealing as I went. The pigs, not me. After I drove on to the ferry, I realized the piglets had been quiet for a long time. I felt a shock of fear that they might have been asphyxiated, locked in the trunk. Opening the trunk was their cue to squeal as loud as they possibly could. One of them had wriggled and poked until all four legs protruded from the burlap sack. It looked like a potato with legs, ready to escape. I shut the trunk just before it could launch out on to the deck. Now there's a picture: a blindfolded pig racing the length of the car deck between the legs of passengers, skittering off the stern of the ferry into Puget Sound and swimming for freedom. You know how people will talk.

As soon as the pigs had gotten settled in at my place, I talked the principal into letting me take one of the pigs to the Middle School where I worked. Even though the school is in a country setting, most kids didn't have animals at home. At any rate, a little pig in the planter well in front of school was good enough reason for half of the student's to miss the first bell.

A key part of this pig raising scheme was getting the students to put their lunch leftovers in a special tub, instead of just chucking it in the garbage. I needed their involvement, so I cooked up a contest to name the pig. No prize, just the honor of having your suggestion picked. After my notice appeared in the

128

school bulletin, entries accumulated rapidly right up to the deadline. The principal, the school secretary and I were the judging committee. The principal wanted to veto any inappropriate entries and I realized that the school secretary runs the whole show and nothing succeeds without her help and approval.

A few entries:

Mr. "P" (Mr. "T" was hot on TV that year)

Bacon Butt (rejected by the principal)

Jimmy Dean

Hamlet (I sneaked that one in anonymously)

Thirteen students submitted the names of other students (remember we are dealing with 7th and 8th graders here). The committee shrugged their collective shoulders and went with "Mr. P"

I drew a cartoon pig with a gaping mouth, placed it over a garbage tub in the cafeteria, and I was in business. Between the finicky eating habits of 14 year olds, the resources of affluent parents, and the government supported school lunch program, I brought home more sandwiches and pizza crusts than two small pigs could imagine eating. It's rare, but a pig will eventually back away from a trough of hamburgers.

Then came an unforeseen problem, Winter Break: No school = no food. Someone recommended using the by-product of the tofu works down the road. Island Spring tofu was glad to give me all the tofu making dregs I could handle, starting with two 40 gallon barrels. I should have known it was going to fail; even prime tofu is barely food anyway, and the leavings resemble sawdust. The pigs sniffed at it and went hungry. The tofu froze solid in the barrels and couldn't even be dumped on the compost heap until warmer weather. I bought them some pig chow from the feed store, but they shunted it back and forth in the trough hoping to find the twinkies and bubble gum of better times. In a pique, they renewed their efforts at undermining my barn by burrowing under the foundation so far that they could sleep in the cave they had excavated with only one little ham protruding.

In spite of the winter weather, Hamlet and Mr."P." were thriving. I decided to move them into the garden tool shed during the coldest weather, but they had grown to 70 pounds, and hadn't been leash-trained yet. Not that I could get a leash to stay on a pig. Observe the pig's physiognomy. It is thick in the middle and tapers to the extremities, and is as hard to put a leash on as a bowling ball. I tried pulling Mr."P" by the front legs, but the hind legs have excellent traction in reverse, plus there is biting. The pig biting me, not the other way around. I hit on picking him up by the hind legs and trundling him along wheelbarrow fashion. It worked! Aside from some very excited comments from the pig, I could really make progress. With his hind legs up, the pig thinks he can run away downhill, and gets those front legs racing. The problem is steering. I hadn't taught them "gee" and "haw" or port and starboard, so they were free to decide where they wanted to go, and you can bet that if I want to go through the tool shed door, a contrary pig will want to make two laps around the shed first.

All school year I had placed a large trash tub near the cafeteria door, with a cartoon image of a smiling pig above.. About two weeks before the end of school I called Gil's Custom Killing and had the pigs butchered.

Back at school. I happened to be standing near the cafeteria door when a girl came up, looked around for the pig's food tub and not finding it, she started to ask ""Where's the:"...her voice trailed off as she caught on. "YOU KILLED MR. P!" she exclaimed. I had to admit it, and my ears burned bright with guilt.

Sailing Down the Inside Passage

"By fleeb peep fbloating poo the thurpluf!"

"What? I can't understand a word you're saying", Mick shouted.

I spat out a mouthful of seawater and said again, "My feet keep floating to the surface!"

Mick, warm and dry in the boat, called back, "I wondered what all that thrashing around was about. Hurry up, you're supposed to be dead from hypothermia by now."

My friend Mick had invited me to sail with him down the Inside Passage of British Columbia in his 21 foot sailboat. A friend had insisted on loaning us two survival suits and we were practicing getting into them on this sunny June day.

Mick has Multiple Sclerosis, and his clumsy legs would not go into the suit, though he made a few half-hearted tries. I was able to hootchie-kootchie into my suit in about 3 minutes, sitting in the boat.

"But can you get into one of these things in the water?", Mick asked.

Overboard I went, survival suit under my arm. As soon as I put my legs into the suit, I immediately floated into a head-down, feet-up position. By holding my breath and wriggling like Houdini, I was able to subdue the suit and sprawl on my back like the shmendrick in the sales brochure. I was pretty comfy, floating in the harbor like a sea otter, except for the 30 gallons of chilly seawater inside the suit. When I attempted to haul myself back into the boat, the water settled down into the feet of the suit, bulging like Popeye's calves, impossible to lift without a windlass. Whoopee-Cushion valves built into the heels let the water drain out slowly while I leaned over the gunnel like a netted halibut.

Aside from Mick's advancing MS, there was another problem: Twink, his teacup of a boat, was built to race across a placid lake to a picnic. But since nearly all of the trip would be inshore sailing, protected from the open ocean by one island after another, I figured the boat could take it. My decision to go or stay really came down to limited vacation time. To get more than ten days off I would have to quit my job as a school custodian. Should I spend the summer chipping gum from the underside of desks or go on the adventure of a lifetime? I suffered over this decision for minutes on end before I decided to go.

Our plan was to trailer the boat north through British Columbia to Prince Rupert, leave the car and trailer, and sail home to Seattle, 600 miles south. Mick would retrieve the car later. After someone else had cleaned gummy desks all summer, I would whine and grovel to get my job back.

It was a liberating feeling to hand in my last time card and turn my mind to planning the journey. Lists ran long but space was short. The first casualty was the inflatable dinghy, Twink's Dink, but when your sailboat is not much bigger than other people's dinghies, it hardly matters. We could run her into shallow water and wade ashore if necessary.

The floppy orange survival suits took up about as much space of a case of whisky, but Mick's wife suggested that taking the suits and leaving the whiskey behind should be viewed as two-for-one accident prevention. We compromised by packing the bottles in the arms and legs of the suits.

On departure day we hitched up the boat and trailer to Mick's beater Chevy sedan and pulled out onto Vashon Island's main drag to swing the compass. Mick lined up the boat more or less in the northbound lane while I tweaked the adjusting screws until the compass agreed that we were headed toward Canada. That two tons of Detroit Iron may have influenced the compass somewhat.

The first leg of our trip was a carefree drive up the wheat and cattle country of eastern B.C. At night we drew surprised stares from the truck drivers, as if they had never seen anyone camping beside the road in a sailboat. I may have gone too far in setting an anchor light, though.

A last westward dash to the coast put us in Prince Rupert. The precipitous hairpin turns and logging trucks make it no place for boat trailering. Assuming you make it, Prince Rupert waits at the end of the road, one of the true nowheres of the world. Is Timbuktu looking for a sister city?

We launched the boat, stashed the car, and bought the last fresh provisions we would have for a while. Shopping for groceries at the Overwaite Supermarket (no kidding), we turned the packaged goods around to read the French side of the label. Petits Pois and Haricots Verts sounded much more haute cuisine and Dinty Moore Pot au Feu was irresistible. While I jammed cabbages, fire extinguishers, muffins, and gas cans into an already filled locker, Mick spoke with the harbormaster who strolled by.

"You fellows going out fishing for the week ?", he asked.

"We'll probably fish all the way down to Seattle."

You're going to Seattle in that? Good luck, but keep your eyes open at Seymour Narrows.

With this left-handed bon voyage we sailed out of the harbor into one of the two dominant weather patterns of coastal B.C.: Threatening To Rain Any Minute; the other being Rain Without End. We sailed south, leaving Prince Rupert astern. I smoked a cigar and Mick wondered aloud how the poor people were doing. Late in the afternoon I scanned my chart and selected a promising anchorage for the night, Blubber Bay. We had just gotten the hook down and dinner started when a whistle shrieked from across the bay and the swing shift commenced at a rock crushing plant. Isn't it remarkable how sound carries across water? You could hear every nuance:

"Sounds like more quartz in tonight's batch, Cecil."

"Yes. I say, isn't that squeal coming from #3 bearing gone dry on the offload belt?

Piloting in the Inside Passage is apprentice's work. You are always in sight of land, if the fog lifts, and most of the channels are wide and deep. Once or twice a day you might have to make a decision about which way to take around an island that had floated into your path. All the navigation charts a real pilot should take for this trip would have displaced our backup case of whiskey, so I was pleased to find a set of charts that had been reduced and laminated in clear plastic and sold as a set of table place mats. The set of four covered a significant part of North America; no matter that entire reefs, torpedo test areas, and submerged wrecks were visible only under a microscope, they fit on the boat and cleaned up well when we spilled chowder on them. I once sailed 15 miles out of our way to avoid a reef of mustard. The compass couldn't make up its mind about where south was without the iron bulk of Mick's Chevy parked in front of it, but no matter, we checked off islands on the placemat as we passed them and got lost only a time or two.

I had two other tools in my pilot's kit, the tide table and the Pacific Coast Pilot. The tide table of the Inside Passage is not the little shirt pocket freebie you pick up at bait shops in the U.S. Most small town phone books have fewer pages than this volume of forgettable lore. Times are given in G.M.T. (Greenwich Mean Time or Zulu time as it is sometimes known) on the 24 hour military clock. Speed and direction of currents are given for hundreds of checkpoints along the coast. I puzzled over the tide table for days and thereafter used it to prop up the dishpan when we were heeled over.

The other troublesome book was the Pacific Coast Pilot, ostensibly a written description of harbors, passages, aids to navigation, and such. While it contains plenty of good advice about getting from a to b, the compilers are at their best describing in daunting, even terrifying, detail every possible menace and hazard to the unwary mariner over 10,000 square miles of navigable water. My favorites are "Unexploded bomb reported 1949, Maelstroms, For full powered vessels only", and the catch-22, "local knowledge required". I expect to find Waikiki Beach listed as foul anchoring ground with occasional threat of tsunamis. We came to call it the Catalog of Nautical Horrors, and resolved that we would have to ignore it regularly or we would neither sail nor anchor anywhere.

The VHF marine weather forecast was similarly gloomy; it was calculated to make a cautious skipper stay in his berth with a blanket over his head, but we listened to it anyway just to hear the Canadians say Soath by Soath-west.

We sailed on by day, anchoring at night with our usual procedure: prowl the perimeter of the prospective anchorage using

137

a fishing pole and sinker to plumb the depth, kick the anchor off the bow, tug on the line to see if it held and give the Happy Hour call, "Anchor Drink!"

We were in wild country with no roads and only here and there a home or an abandoned cannery. We got to taking the average magnificent fjord with pristine waterfall pretty much in stride. A little hidey-hole farther down the chart fascinated me: God's Pocket.

The real life of the area was on the water. Daily we passed fishing boats, car ferries, and yachts that probably used gold bars for ballast. Once, in a narrow channel we met Noordam, a cruise ship that filled our field of vision as its towering sides swept past. With uplifted faces we saw tennis players swatting balls on net-enclosed upper deck courts, occasionally missing a volley when they were distracted by the sight of little Twink rolling and bucking in the ship's wake.

A week out on the trip we began to feel the lack of life's luxuries.

I called down to Mick in the cabin, "What's that low tide smell in there?"

"I'm making Cream of Leftovers for dinner. You Want some green bread with that?"

With my mantra, "cheeseburgers and dry socks" fixed in mind, I anticipated our arrival at Bella Bella, an Indian village mentioned in the Pilot.

So far we had kept good company with seals, and bald eagles. In Canada our Majestic National Bird gets about as much respect as a sea gull. Quite often the first indication we had of nearby civilization was an eagle circling the village dump, competing for garbage with the gulls. Dump Eagles told me Bella Bella must be around the next headland. I was surprised to see the dozen shacks painted in colors a Jamaican would be too shy to use, all the hot colors, tropical fruit pastels and mismatches from a surplus paint auction. The exception was the Bella Bella Band Store, camouflaged as patchy fog.

Mick and I looked over the modest stock of goods on sale while the idlers kept a fishy eye on us. Perhaps the band chamber of commerce sponsors a Welcome Wagon:

"Hi. Here. (hands over a basket of canned fruit from the band store.)

Mind your own business and there won't be any trouble."

There were no cheeseburgers to be had, but they did have the world's thickest, woolliest boot socks. Dry too! Mick selected a raincoat unknown at Eddie Bauer, designer rainwear by Helly Hansen of Norway. It came down to nearly ankle length and was made of heavy, sea-green rubberized canvas. He chose it because he couldn't get rain pants on and off. I didn't have to dare him to top it off with the sou'wester straight out of Captains Courageous; he already had it on. Outside in the drizzle, with Mick's stiff-legged walk, the raincoat looked like a slithering, lurching pile of kelp. It is normally impossible to unfreeze a Bella Bellan, but I'm pretty sure I saw one smirk that day.

I admit I have a thing for floatplanes, and especially the DeHavilland Otter (the Flying Whale). Their distinctive feature is a Pratt and Whitney 600 hp radial engine that makes my gizzard tingle when it starts up. We always heard their growl before we saw them. Sandwiched between low clouds and the water, they grumbled by, just above mast height, banked sharply around the bend and left us to waddle along our course alone. They are the UPS trucks of coastal B.C.

Our next destination was Dawson's Landing. Owing to the steep fjord walls, very little of this outpost was on shore. Instead, an acre of log rafts supported the store, some cabins, and a fuel shack. As veteran sailors, we had by now learned to keep well clear of the dock spaces marked for float planes, and a timely lesson it was too, for we had just stepped ashore with our mooring lines when an Otter performed a record short and steep landing, stopping just two feet from the dock. The pilot popped his door open and in one motion, stepped from float to the dock and tied up with that casual knot that Roy Rogers used when he rode up to the sheriff's office. By the time his breathless passengers fumbled their door open, the pilot had their duffels, fishing rods and the Canada Post bags chucked out on the dock. The woman in charge (perhaps Mrs. Dawson?) handed over the outbound mail, the Otter accelerated in a gale of spray and skipped into the air. One of the sport fishermen turned slowly, scanning the scene like a lighthouse and asked me "Is this Dawson's Landing?" Out of an inherited perverse sense of humor I answered "Nope".

Once the new arrivals had been ushered into the cafe, the proprietress spoke to me in front of her store. "You didn't come up through Seymour Narrows in that did you?"

"No, we're headed south that way."

Oh Lord! Just make sure you go through at slack tide and you'll be OK, probably."

My placemat chart showed Seymour Narrows as the day's next attraction. I made a last attempt to decipher the tide book and determined that we would be going through either at dead slack or maximum flood, or somewhere in between. I put the tide table back under the dish pan.

As we neared the narrows, I could not see if there really was a pass at all, just high canyon walls. We were making great progress and gaining speed, but the source was the current, not our expert sail trim.

I should mention that we had, clamped to the transom, a flea market Monkey Ward outboard motor. When both cylinders were working, it was fine for maneuvering in a harbor, but it was not the long-shaft sailboat model. Consequently, in just a little chop, the propeller would lift out of the water and make a fine rackety rooster-tail without moving the boat. Now, when we needed it, I was relieved when I got it started on the second pull. Mick and I took our places in the cockpit, listening only to the ZZZZZZZ of the motor. We were ready for anything.

ZZZZZZZZZpoppityZZZZZZZZZ.

There is no optimist alive who can have faith in a motor that throws in the occasional "poppity".

The current continued to gain speed. Upwelling water made humps in the surface of the flow. I realized that we could not have turned around and powered back against the rushing water. Our ticket for Seymour Narrows had been punched. Unseen countercurrents leaned against our keel, overpowering our rudder. Mick sat with both hands clamped on the tiller, eyes staring straight ahead.

"This doesn't look like slack tide", I said. A great lazy back-eddy generated by a granite ledge jutting out from shore pushed our bow 90 degrees off course. We saw, clearly now, the bottleneck of the pass only a hundred yards ahead. The center third was occupied by a whirlpool four boatlengths wide.

Poppity ZZZZZZ poppity.

As I watched in disbelief, it seemed that Mick had decided to turn around and shoot the pass stern first. "Mick, what the hell are you doing?"

He was cast in the usual steering position, and answered vacantly, "I don't know." We were now in the bottleneck and firmly in the grip of the whirlpool. "Give me the tiller", I howled, resisting the urge to throw him overboard. Now I was the one steering backward in the roiling river. The whirlpool didn't want to let us go, but carried us right around. We were going back north! For all the good my steering did, we could have stopped and had a fine fistfight.

The usually stoic Mick glared at me with an eye for mayhem. One more caprice of the whirlpool positioned us to go through the pass again , this time sideways.

Poppity poppity---- poot.

I cursed the motor and waved the tiller back and forth ineffectually, but the whirlpool decided to let us go with no consideration of my efforts. With a last wash of the current we were through. Mick and I sat without speaking, letting the boat drift along in the decelerating current of the widening channel. I remember making a conscious effort to breathe.

Our next few days of idyllic sailing brought us into civilized country. The rain let up and at the next town I learned how to read the tide table. We grew accustomed to finding cheeseburgers and dry socks on every street corner and for the next 200 miles we might as well have been daysailing in front of downtown Seattle.

Nowadays, when some novice sailor barges across my right of way, I shout, "Placemat Navigator!"

Mrs. Ella Schalansky

I ran this story through Fib Check on the computer and it came out 73% true with the remainder divided between writer's license and bona fide lies.

My 8th grade vocal music teacher had fallen so far from greatness and glory that only now, after 35 years, could I properly feel her losses. Rumor spoke of her career as an opera diva and pet of the European music critics when this century was new. But in 1960 Mrs. Schalansky needed two canes to creak down the halls of Eureka Junior High to face her fate teaching vocal music to 8th graders in a remote Northern California mill town. The Crowned Heads of Europe were seldom seen here.

Age had crumpled her down so that from her position at the grand piano, I could see only her head above the lid, eyes glaring out at the world through thick, magenta tinted glasses, her face a mask of powder furrowed with wrinkles. Her hair was always tightly braided and wound into a tall cone fastened to the top of her head with long Chinese hairpins.

I have been condemned to one semester of vocal music through some machination of the Cabala in the faculty room. The third period bell rings, and a stern glance from Mrs. Schalansky cows us into our places on the risers. Bitterness and physical pain have consolidated her range of expression to the Stern Glance and the Dismissive Wave. The Stern Glance translates into "Straighten Up". If you don't, she turns away from you and waves her hand toward the door in a gesture that sweeps you out of the room. She is from the Old School, perhaps before the Old School, the one that regarded Woodrow Wilson as a flibbertigibbet.

Today the class is being tested for vocal range. Each student is expected to advance toward the piano and sing out loud, do, re, mi, fa, so, et cetera. This is a breeze for most of the girls. They stand up straight, hold their hands in a ladylike pose and sing right out in their young soprano voices. And then they ask if they can try it again. The number of boys who ask to give it another go could be counted on the fingers of an oyster.

Madame Schalansky has been going down the roll book in alphabetical order and is getting terrifyingly close to the "F"s. Fridley. Though it is distinctly Freedl pronounced in her old world accent.

"Erlwine. Come".

Chuckie Erlwine doesn't do too badly. He homes in on a couple of the baritone notes, hits his stride , and goes for the top. "Fa, sol, la, ti, dawk". Cut down by the mid-puberty voice break, Erlwine retreats, ears pulsing crimson, eyes cast down to his Keds.

I am oblivious to Erlwein's ordeal. I am dizzy and my shorts are in a bunch.

"Freedl"

I am electrocuted by the sound of my name.

"Stop your viggling."

What? Am I spared? It's not my turn! She was only scolding me for squirming and hyperventilating audibly.

"Finnegan. Come"

Finnegan also would rather be stretched on the rack. His

little choirboy voice hasn't got a note lower than a canary chirp. He is still the chubby little boy I knew in 6th grade. Finnegan gets placed with the alto girls but seeps down through the cracks in the floorboards before he can make it back to the risers.

It was Finnegan who once pointed out to me Mrs. Schalansky's shiny 1940 Plymouth toiling down the street in low gear, as always. We knew it was her because the sedan appeared to be piloted by a tall cone of braided hair skewered with lacquered chopsticks.

"Freedl. Come."

I am a bodiless entity floating high above the classroom looking down on my physical self as I stumble on senseless feet toward the piano. I ask for a blindfold and a last cigarette before the darkness comes.

After Christmas vacation, Mrs. Schalansky wasn't there anymore. I walked into the old high-ceilinged classroom, expecting to find Mrs. Schalansky among the other Victorian architectural fixtures, and she was not there. In her place was Miss Downing, beautiful, just out of college and with music in her voice.

I helped her sort through those cheerless, hidebound old songbooks, boxed them up and dumped them in a closet at the back of the room. Next day she brought in some of her own sheet music; music with PEP in it.

I'm gonna sit right down and write myself a letter, Oh Yeah!,

and pretend that every one's from you oo.oo

Do you hear that whirring sound

way down underneath the ground

It's the Victorian Era

spinning around. I hear ya!

Out with the Old Guard.

In with the Avant Garde. Yeah !

Boodley op'm bebop

Ba doo boo bah.

Yeah!

It was a new world.

I never asked what happened to Mrs. S, nor thought much, until now, about my brief exposure to life as it was for the Old School and the respect that was required of young people a hundred years ago.

The Dirt Report
6-29-98

Last Day of School

By staring at the calendar intently for two weeks, I made the last day of school arrive . The last day or two were an exercise in keeping the lid on a classroom full of very squirrelly 7th graders. Showing "Flubber" in class was a good move, but, still, half of the class didn't have the attention span for it. The school held an outdoor BBQ and field day that was a big hit, especially the mud-wrestling pit. The P.E. teachers made a pond out of hay bales and visquine sheet and filled it 6" deep with top quality mud. Boys could challenge boys, girls challenged girls and the waiting list filled immediately. Even a few of the Fashion Princesses gave it a go. The faculty stood around pretending not to have prurient interest. The girl's P.E. teacher got the job of sluicing the contestants down with a fire hose. 45 degree water, screams of shock. Cool, dude.

Motorhoming in our own back yard.

Our neighbors loaned us their 20' motorhome and we took off for five days on a trip through the adjacent county, stopping at a resort on the Straits for two days. I recommend the beautiful county parks up here. Early in the season they were thinly populated and offered good beachcombing and tidepool exploring . The A-frame cabin we stayed in was nicely furnished, right on the beach, but not much bigger than the motorhome. Kathyrn got skunked, fishing in some spectacular settings. RVers be warned, most of the drive is snaky, 35 m.p.h., slowing to 15 at the hairpin turns. Logging Truck Road Racing in effect 20 hrs. a day.

149

Neah Bay, the only village on the Makah Indian reservation, is an odd mix. The Cultural Museum is lavish, the Coast Guard station is stark, and the General store, remote as it is, tries to carry everything you need, from stovepipe to lipstick. The rest of the village seems to be a collection of sleeping dogs, dirt roads, ruined mobile homes and wrecked pickup trucks. I wonder if those dogs bite? Better let sleeping dogs lie.

Angel of the Airwaves

Kathyrn is in Seattle for 4 or 5 weeks, working as a broadcaster for the Radio For The Blind. The learning curve is abrupt because of the many opportunities for technical glitches, but she does a good job of maintaining that beautiful, unruffled radio voice.

Hard Hat Blues

I was roaming around in Port Angeles last week when I thought to stop in at a ship repair office to check out employment.

"Is this the office where hiring is done?", I asked the woman behind the desk.

"Sure is, but you'll need a long sleeve shirt and boots. Can you be back in 15 minutes?

That's how I learned I was a welder's helper.

It turned out o be a two-day job repairing a crack in a tired old oil tanker. Denali, at age 25, needed crack welds every couple of months. The petroleum hold is emptied and ventilated, a chemist comes aboard to certify that the air inside won't blow up or kill you right away, and the workers are allowed to enter.

Certified it may be, but it sho' do stink! Stand around for half an hour, do a little work, stand around some more, go home 12 hours later, bored out of your skull. My bonehead students were right; you don't need to learn anything in school, as long as you have a high tolerance for grunt work and boredom.

Having successfully identified one more career I don't care for, I am hopeful for better things to come.

Your pal,

Neal

Merry Christmas

December, 1997

Dear Friends,

Merry Christmas from Neal and Kathyrn Fridley

It has been a great year. Our Microsoft stock has done pretty well for us, so I've decided to bag the working thing and pursue some other options. The flying lessons have been a blast. Kathyrn hopes to wind down her research at the Laboratory. There's talk of a Nobel prize for her team. The twins are doing well at Harvard and little Fannie is taking a year off to do some grant writing for the Mother Theresa Foundation... Wait a minute... Whoa!...Hold the phone...Where did that come from? My mind has been working like a slot machine lately. I pull the lever and I never know what will come up. Let's take another stab at this.

Happy Holidays from Us at The Dirt

No dawn today, just a lighter shade of gray to the cloud cover. I'm sorry to see the colors fade to muted shades. No snow yet. There goes my developing theory of snowfall by Turkey Day. Last year, an un-Nin~o year, we were snowed in for three days at year end. I rammed my 4wd truck at the snow on our road for hours to push through to the county road. Kathyrn drove our little town car up from Seattle in a New Year's Eve storm and made it to within a quarter mile of home before a big snowbank jumped out from behind a bush and ate the car. When she showed up at the door, looking like a friendly polar bear, I got up off the warm couch to go dig the car out. Later she claimed I made disparaging remarks about her driving, but in my defense, I was lying under the car in an ice puddle at the time. My wish this year is that we will be here together for the holidays.

On Turning 50

I was feeling kind of punk about this birthday until I spotted a book titled, "Oh To Be 50 Again", and decided to stop whining. For my 50th birthday Kathyrn and her longtime bud, Deidra, treated me to a trip to Nashville and Deidra's home, Atlanta. Deidra, the one-woman welcoming throng, met us at the airport. As a greeter, she is equal to a small brass band and a dozen baton twirlers. The other travelers no doubt wished some one would have shown up for them wearing a Viking helmet and waving balloons. Her balloon that read "Older than Dirt" has been my 50th year banner. I also wish to pass on this news from our kind friend LouOma: on your 50th, you get to celebrate the whole year, not just a day.

Deidra drove us a "short hop" of 300 miles to her home near Atlanta, leaving me free to watch the limestone hills and hardwood forests roll by, at least as much as could be seen between the convoys of trucks that surrounded us. Living as I do up here at the spur-end of the Interstate Highway system, I hadn't imagined the extent of the truck stop culture we found on the New York-Atlanta corridor. We pulled in to a 15 acre Truck-0-Rama to sample the cuisine: Biscuits and gravy at the cafe, of course, and an "RC Co-Coler" and a Moon Pie at the mini-Mart. Coke and Pepsi have all but pushed RC off the shelf, and a Moon Pie, I found, is a bland, air-filled cookie, but Deidra led us to the real gold, Goo-Goo Bars, a chocolate and nut cluster. Before leaving the truck stop, I had to check out the gambling machines (they pay off in scrip), TV room (a dozen sleepy truck drivers watching soaps), barber shop, and Laundromat. You can live your life on the Interstate with only an occasional need to exit for weddings and funerals.

Banana Trees in the Sauna.

Deidra and Kathyrn promoted the visit to the Atlanta Arboretum, but I was the one who enjoyed the best part of it. The Jungle Conservatory is a four story glass enclosure containing a tropical rain forest. I opened the door to go in and a great billow of steam rolled out as if from a shower stall. The ladies considered the hair-frizz factor and balked, so I went in alone. I could feel my lungs expand and contract, but I couldn't tell if there was any actual air mixed in with the steam. It was a delight to experience the jungle without the danger of being eaten by bugs or jaguars, though a particularly nasty looking plant seemed to eye me as a possible source of protein.

The Search for Georgia Bobba-Q

We didn't have to search very hard. We found barbecue on every street corner, like liquor stores in California. The funkiest one we went to was a joint on Peachtree Street (That won't help you find it; there are 15 Streets, Lanes, Boulevards, etc. named "Peachtree" in Atlanta). Be prepared for deep-fried sweet potatoes (topped with powdered sugar), chili fries, and Brunswick stew. This last item is definitely not from New Brunswick, Canada, but a gumbo-culture island on the Georgia coast. Y'all come back and see us, now.

3000 Rednecks in Denim Leisure Suits

The three of us went to the Grand Ole Opry in Nashville. The Opry show began in the late twenties as live entertainment, but is now more of a musical museum. The performers had their hits 30 or 40 years ago and stayed with a good thing. Grandpa Jones (or his mummy) came out and wheezed through "That

Good Old Mountain Dew". Another fossil, Little Jimmy Dickens, or the nubbin that was left of him, came out to do his turn. He stood a smidge taller than his Martin Dreadnought guitar, if you count his hat. "Skeeter Davis and Ray Price, how's it been goin' the last 30 years? Porter Waggoner, are all the grandchirren doin' good?"

This live radio show rolls along on well greased tracks. Performers enter and leave the stage while the announcer introduces the next act. "The Grand Ole Opry Show is broadcast live ever Satiddy night on WSM, 650 on your radio dial. Before we bring on the rest of our show, you've got just enough time to get on down to the concession stand for a good ol' Goo-Goo bar. Everybody loves a Goo-Goo."

Del Reeves came out near the close of the show to sing his hit "My Rose of San Antone". He reached out into the audience and sang directly to Kathyrn's heart. After the show, as the crowd ebbed out of the theater, Kathyrn danced and twirled in a world of her own, singing that song. Since then she and our neighbors, Larry and Sandy Smith have adopted the song and sing it whenever inspiration strikes.

Convergence at the DIRT.

For a second year, Kathyrn hosted a women's party in August that has come to be known as the Perseid Meteor Shower and Convergence at The Dirt. She wishes to report that the Chinese paper lanterns in the late summer evening were memorable and the porta-potty rented from La Pooh was an added touch of civility this year. As before, the wood-fired hot tub did not lack for stokers and soakers. Of course, each participant assumed that no one else would bring enough food, so the 30 square foot table I had set up could not hold all the provisions.

Sub Dude

My second year of substitute teaching feels more like biz as usual and less like last year's panic. In September there isn't much work; the teachers are determined and healthy, but by Thanksgiving the ranks are weakened and decimated. My first teaching assignment of the year was due to a kind of family bereavement leave. The auto shop teacher called in an emergency absence when he discovered his family's horse, Ginger, dead in the pasture. His kids had all grown up riding her, and now that her time had come, the teacher wanted to get her buried before the kids got home from school. At 16 hands, Ginger was no pony. He had to rent a backhoe and bury her where she lay. I have buried a few of my own pets, so I know what it is to dig a pet's grave while your eyes fill with tears. Pet's funerals are hard enough without having to rent a backhoe.

This year's teaching assignments haven't been entirely routine. I taught 7 days at Opportunity Alternative Middle School and struggled every minute of it. In theory, Opportunity is set up for students who don't do well in the mainstream middle schools.. It has the unenviable reputation of being a holding pen for losers, flunk-outs, druggies, the picked-on and the pickers. While parts of that are difficult to deny at first glance, I say that the courage required just to get up in the morning and stay straight enough to make it to school is extraordinary. Collect a month's worth of newspaper clippings about crimes against children and domestic violence and you have the family album for these kids. When a Judge says, "Son, either you go to jail or you go school", he means Opportunity.. One thing the students have in common is the psychological maturity of 4th graders. The inability to trust others makes them loners at a time when other kids are learning life lessons about friendship. At the regular schools I see students lugging their band instruments to school or excitedly boarding a

157

bus to play a basketball game at another school. At Opportunity, Rehab and Probation are the extracurricular activities.

I came home at the end of each day feeling that I'd have better success teaching long division to a flock of geese. Geese would run around, make a lot of noise, pick on each other, and still not understand long division, but at least they would not whine about how boring and dumb it was. My students frequently told me that the lesson was stupid, impossible, and they would never get it. I privately wrote them off as losers. I felt that trying to teach them anything was impossible and a waste of time. The revelation that came to me in the middle of all this was that my own attitude was loser thinking. After that, my last two days there were happier. I was content to chip away where I could and celebrate even very small successes.

Is Everybody On The Bus?

Substitute teaching is as close as you can get to being unemployed and still have a job. Even then summer rolled around and I had to find a real job. Unfortunately, none were available, so I drove for Northwest Jitney Service for the summer. I showed up for my first day of work at the company headquarters, which was also the owner's house. Three phones rang continually, deadlines came and went in last minute scrambles and tension and confusion filled in the gaps. Everyone apologized for the extraordinary disorganization, but, as I later learned, that was the customary mode of operation. Herb, the owner, gave me a briefing on the day's passenger list. "Let's see, It looks like you'll be full going in to Seattle. Gee, look at this! Sorry to hit you with three C.B.R.s on your first day."

"C.B.R.s ? Is that bad?"

"Clallam Bay Prison Releasees. They just got out of Clallam Bay Prison."

Oh, great, I thought. Yesterday they were unfit to mingle with free people and today they're riding my bus, eying my cash pouch.

Herb said "Just don't let them sit next to any children or offer to carry any old ladies' purses. You'll be OK; we've only been robbed once."

It was true; a C.B.R. had robbed a driver and 30 minutes later robbed a bank.

The secretary reminded us, "Isn't Jittery John supposed to supposed to ride with us today?

Herb realized the oversight and explained the problem. Jittery John rides with us every Wednesday to a drug Rehab clinic in Seattle. "He might get a little jumpy toward the end of the trip, but don't worry, he's never hurt anyone. But that's not the real challenge. You're overbooked, so unless you have some no-shows, somebody will have to be booted off in Sequim. Give 'em a buck to take City Transit back home and tell 'em we're sorry."

He handed me the keys to the bus. "Oops, wrong keys. Oops again, bus #3 lost its transmission yesterday. You'd better take # 5, but fuel up before you go...it's empty. Better get moving, you're supposed to be at your first stop in two minutes."

Yaaaaahhhh.

So far, I haven't been robbed, Jittery John hasn't flipped out, and I've only run the bus out of fuel once with passengers aboard. Herb says he will try to get the fuel gauge fixed as soon

159

as some extra money shows up.

The real reward for coping with all this horsepuckey is the people you meet:

The Indian grandma headed for Sitka with four suitcases and a 15 horse outboard motor. She was going to join her kids at their summer fishing camp.

The four Swiss steelhead fishermen, homeward bound and debating what to tell their wives about their vacation. They sometimes lowered their voices and lapsed into German and laughed at the juicy parts. They looked so tame to me. What could they have been up to? Probably overeating.

Pastor Ralph met me at the P.A. bus stop and handed over to my care 8 Chinese high school girls and their 8 identical mega-suitcases. Each one weighed 90 pounds, all hard cases, with straps all over them...the suitcases , not the girls. One of them seemed to have been around a little more than the others... the girls, not the suitcases, and acted as spokeswoman. At the ferry dock, where I collect the fares, the girls handed me their Greyhound Ameripass tickets.

Uh-oh. "These no good", I signed. "I need twenty dollars". Their little Asian eyes opened up round when I explained that I meant twenty dollars each. The best English speaker asked if travelers checks were OK. "Sure", I said, so they trooped up to the front of the bus to sign the checks in my presence, as required.

These letters are a little unfamiliar to me. That first one could be a two-story dog house. The second one looks like a cracked window. Is the last one a chicken's foot? "Girls, we can forgo the signature check. Just sign the checks and give them to me. I'm sure our bookkeeper won't quibble with travelers checks drawn on the Hong Feng bank of Shanghai."

Radio Free Bosnia

Kathyrn worked as an on-call broadcaster for the Radio for the Blind in Seattle. For a year they operated out of temporary quarters in a cramped, hot little room jammed with haywire audio equipment. Not many people smiled when I called it Radio Free Bosnia. Later on,when construction was complete, Evergreen Radio Reading Service (its real name) hit its stride and became a great place to work.

They do live interviews, read newspaper articles, and tap into a national network for syndicated programs, all with only one broadcaster on duty. The day staff records and cues up the automated tape decks for unattended nighttime operation. Most of the 8 million buttons in the room have the potential to screw things up royally, so Kathyrn's learning curve was steep and bumpy. Think of Lucy and Ethel trying to keep up with the candy conveyor belt. Their new building was eventually completed and no one misses the old one. When I visited, Kathyrn sat in a cool, carpeted, softly lit studio that looked like a control room on a Star Wars set.

Kathyrn Loses Bid For Queen of the Weed Board

Kathyrn heard about a part-time job with a new branch of the county government that oversees weed control. Not exactly glamorous, but around here you would be lucky to get a steady job in your interest area. Certainly Kathyrn's Weed War here at The Dirt should count as interest and experience. In a ploy to strengthen her resume, she signed up for the WSU Master Gardener course, ten days of classes that led to a certificate issued by the county agriculture office. In the end, she didn't get the Weed Board job, but the class turned out to be a great way to meet new friends with common interests.

That's all the ore I can dig out of the Story Mine. If there's any nuggets in there, you'll hafta high-grade 'em out yourself.

A New Bike for an Old Duffer

When I was about to turn 40 I walked into a bicycle shop and said to the salesman, "I can't ride in that leaned-over racing position any more. My back doesn't like it and speed isn't my main goal. I need to ride in a more upright position, even if I look like an old duffer."

The young salesman said, "I've got what you need right here- the Roadburner 5000". He showed me a bike with handlebars that were raised a little higher than most, but not even close to the height I hoped for.

"You're not getting the picture", I said. "I want to ride sitting almost upright. And I want a seat that is comfortable, not this little rail here. This seat feels like carved hickory with some vinyl glued over it." I looked at the tires. They were the diameter of a wiener, which was some improvement over the ones the size of your little finger, but they were still hard as cast iron.

"And while I'm at it," I asked, "when are bicycles going to get suspension? Motorcycles have had spring suspension since my Dad was a pup."

I must have been raising my voice because another young salesman came over and spoke, "Hey, man, I know where they got a bike like you want"

I looked at him expectantly.

"Out at the Mall, man, at Toys R Us."

It was his snicker that got me. You probably read about it in the newspapers, "Two Salesmen Found Strangled in Bike Shop. No Apparent Motive". OK, I admit, I did it, but no jury of my peers would convict me.

So I bought a new bike last month, and it brought a feeling of smug self-righteousness because, guess what? All the Young Lions who designed bicycles years ago have turned 50 and gotten weak in the knees and stiff in the back. They re-designed bicycles and even re-wrote the brochures, i.e. "With little loss in speed and power the new breed of bicycles offer comfort and an ergonomic riding position". After all these years! Hooray!

The seat on my new bike is broad and soft. Spring loaded suspension in the seat post and forks take the jolt and hammer out of riding on rough roads. The handlebars are way up in the air where I need them. And those skinny little tires that would falter over a pebble? Leave them to the all-out racers. My new tires are wide enough to work well on dirt roads and give that "marshmallow ride"

Having a new bike inspires me to go adventuring on it, but I am hesitant to blurt out any big plans. It's like getting a new pencil and announcing that you intend to write a great novel with it. Still, Highway 101 runs right through Port Angeles and doesn't end until it reaches Mexico.

Happy Trails,

Neal

December 2003

Thank you for buying my book. If you liked it, tell your friends. I mean that! Email your friends and let them know where to buy the book. That's what it takes to make my work a success. If you don't like the book, tell me. In fact, all comments, positive and negative, can be directed to me at nfridley@olypen.com .